MW01443158

AN AIR FORCE ATTORNEY'S PERSONAL STORY OF
SMILES, LAUGHTER, TEARS, AND FEARS SERVING IN IRAQ AND AFGHANISTAN

BULLETS BATHROOMS & BAD GUYS

MEMOIRS FROM MY TIME IN AN IRAQI PRISON

By Hugh Spires, Jr.

Bullets, Bathrooms & Bad Guys: Memoirs from my time in an Iraqi prison

Copyright © 2021 Hugh Spires, Jr.

All rights reserved. This is the sole work of the author, and no portion of this publication may be copied or re-published in any publication without express permission of the publisher or author.

ISBN: 9798461149574

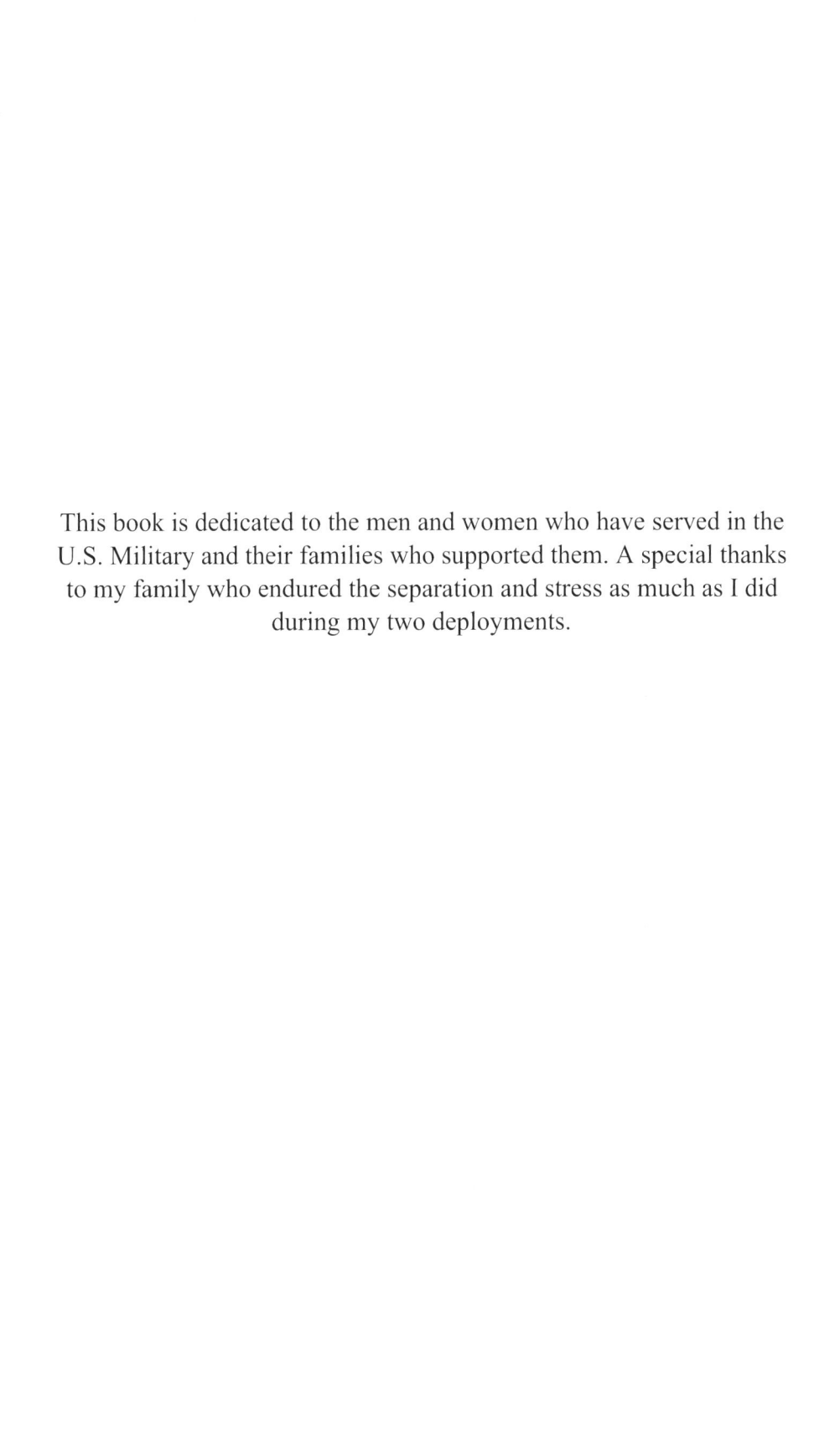

This book is dedicated to the men and women who have served in the U.S. Military and their families who supported them. A special thanks to my family who endured the separation and stress as much as I did during my two deployments.

TABLE OF CONTENTS

PREFACE i
GLOSSARY iii

PART I: HEADING TO WAR

INTRODUCTION 1
LEAVING ON A JET PLANE 11
    October 5, 2004. Tuesday 11
    October 6, 2004. Wednesday 12
    October 8, 2004. Friday 13
COMING IN, HOT OR NOT 15
ORDERED TO PRISON 19
    October 9, 2004. Saturday 20
OUTSIDE THE WIRE 21
    October 10, 2004. Sunday 25
HEADING TO COURT 27

PART II: TIME IN PRISON

HEADING TO PRISON 37
    October 11, 2004. Monday 37
ARRIVING AT ABU 39
MEETING MY TEAM 47
THE JOB 49
THE ATTACKS BEGIN 53
    October 13, 2004. Wednesday 53
    October 14, 2004. Thursday 53
GETTING THE LAYOUT 55
INSIDE THE WALLS OF ABU 59
THE PERKS OF PRISON 63
    October 15, 2004. Friday 63

WAKE UP CALL	67
October 16, 2004. Saturday	67
October 17, 2004. Sunday	68
October 18, 2004. Monday	69
October 19, 2004. Tuesday	71
THE GHETTO HAS A VISITOR	73
October 20-21, 2004. Wed-Thurs	73
October 22, 2004. Friday	74
SPACE INVADERS	75
October 23, 2004. Saturday	76
PROBLEMS IN THE OFFICE	79
TIGHTENING UP	81
October 27, 2004. Wednesday	82
OBLIGATORY THRONE SHOT	83
READING THE TEA LEAVES	87
October 29, 2004. Friday	87
REAL BLOOD FOR HALLOWEEN	89
October 31, 2004. Sunday	89
ESCAPE ATTEMPT	93
November 3, 2004. Wednesday	93
November 4, 2004. Thursday	95
SHARING THE TOILET	97
November 6, 2004. Saturday	97
PREPARING FOR THE TOWER	99
November 9, 2004. Tuesday	99
TIME IN THE TOWER	101
November 10, 2004. Wednesday	101
DRESSING DOWN	109
November 12, 2004. Friday	109

November 14, Sunday 112
MORE DEATHS 113
November 16, 2004. Tuesday 114
CHANGES IN THE OFFICE 115
NATURE NIGHT CALLS 117
SMALL WORLD 119
November 17, 2004. Wednesday 120
VISITING SADDAM 123
CLIENTS IN THE DESERT 125
TRAVEL TIME 127
November 19, 2004. Friday 127
TRAVELING NERVES 129
November 22, 2004. Monday 130
GOING TO COURT AGAIN 131
BACK TO PRISON 135
November 28, 2004. Sunday 135
THE MARINE GRIPES 139
THE BAD GUYS 143
December 6, 2004. Monday 145
SADDAM'S HEARING 147
December 7, 2004. Tuesday 147
PRISONERS ESCAPED 151
FLYING AND DYING 153
December 10, 2004. Friday 153
December 15, 2004. Wednesday 155
MAKING PLANS FOR THE HOLIDAYS 157
December 16, 2004. Thursday 157
HOLLYWOOD MEETS REALITY 159
December 19, 2004, Sunday 159

CALLING HOME FOR CHRISTMAS 161
ONE STRANGE MOOD.. 163
    December 22, 2004. Wednesday 163
SANTA'S COMING 165
    December 23, 2004. Thursday.. 165
    December 27, 2004. Monday.. 166
A LITTLE SURGERY 171
    December 28, 2004. Tuesday 171
    December 29, 2004. Wednesday 172
POST HOLIDAY BLUES 175
    December 31, 2004. Friday.. 175
WAR TROPHIES 179
    January 1, 2005. Saturday.. 179
    January 5, 2005. Wednesday 179
RECORD OF ATTACKS 181
THE TORTURE TOUR 183
    January 6, 2005. Thursday... 184
KINKS IN THE CHAIN... 185
    January 7, 2005. Friday... 187
PRISONER ESCAPE 189
    January 10, 2005. Monday... 189
    January 11, 2005. Tuesday 190
GETTING CLOSER.. 191
WATCHING DETAINEE INTERROGATIONS 193
    January 12, 2005. Wednesday 193
CRACKS IN THE OFFICE... 195
    January 13, 2005. Thursday... 195
    January 14, 2005. Friday... 199
CHINESE TAKE-OUT IN BAGHDAD 201

January 18, 2005. Tuesday 201
January 20, 2005. Thursday 202
A WAKE-UP CALL 203
January 21, 2005. Friday 203
FIRE FIGHTS AND NEWS REPORTING 209
January 26, 2005. Wednesday 209
January 27, 2005. Thursday 211
TENSIONS FLARE 213
January 28, 2005. Friday 214
ELECTION WITH A BANG 217
January 30, 2005. Sunday 217
February 1, 2005. Thursday 218

PART III: HEADING HOME

COMING HOME 223
February 7, 2005. Monday 223
HITCHHIKING ACROSS KUWAIT 225
TO THE HILTON HOTEL, PLEASE 229
THE LONG FLIGHT HOME 231
February 10, 2005. Thursday 231
CONCLUSION 233

PROLOGUE

AFGHANISTAN 237
ABOUT THE AUTHOR 253

PREFACE

This story is about overcoming the fear of being killed in combat, with a smile on your face. When a person thinks of soldiers fighting a war, they don't often think of military attorneys, called JAGs. My story is one of smiles, laughter, tears, and fears. I wrote this book to give the reader a perspective of an attorney's time in Iraq and Afghanistan facing daily mortars and threats while performing the job. Each person's experience in a combat zone is different. My account is not intended to compare my experiences with soldiers on the front line or make light of a serious and deadly war that took the lives of many good Americans. The purpose of this book is to share my experience as an Air Force JAG in two combat zones and show how having a laugh can make the threat of death less worrisome. Perhaps others going through a stressful or dangerous situation can see how effective the approach can be. I hope you enjoy it!

GLOSSARY

BIAP: Baghdad International Airport

CRRB: Combined Review & Release Board. A board consisting of Iraqi and U.S. soldiers who determine whether a detainee is a security threat, should be prosecuted in the court, or released.

CCCI: Central Criminal Court of Iraq. Consists of three Iraqi judges who sit as a panel to determine whether a detainee is guilty of committing a crime and the appropriate punishment.

DFAC: Dining Facility

GITMO: Guantanamo Bay, Cuba

ICO: Iraqi Correctional Officer. Guard prisoners who have violated laws of Iraq.

IED: Improvised Explosive Device. Home-made bombs assembled and detonated by Iraqis to harm U.S. soldiers.

JAG: Judge Advocate General. Licensed attorneys who represent the military in various matters such as criminal prosecution, contract law, employment law, medical law, environment law, and military operations law.

JIDC: Joint Interrogation and Debriefing Center. Responsible for conducting interviews of detainees to exploit intelligence information.

MEF: Marine Expeditionary Force

MEPS: Military Entrance Processing Station

MP: Military Policeman

MRE: Meal Ready to Eat. Self-contained field ration used for meals that can be heated without fire.

MWR: Military Welfare and Recreation. Responsible for quality-of-life programs for military members.

NCOIC: Non-Commissioned Officer in Charge. Senior ranking enlisted member in a group with supervisory responsibilities.

NIPR: Non-Secured Internet Protocol Router. Computer access used to communicate non-classified information.

OIC: Officer in Charge. Senior ranking officer in a group with supervisory responsibilities.

SIPR: Secured Internet Protocol Router. Computer access used to communicate classified information.

TCN/HCN: Third Country National/Host Country National.

TNA: Transition National Assembly. Elected government officials from Iraqi provinces.

UXO: Unexploded Ordinance. Explosives such as mortars that have failed to completely explode.

VBIED: Vehicle Borne Improvised Explosive Device. Also, known as a car bomb that is often used in suicide missions.

PART I

HEADING TO WAR

INTRODUCTION

It is a rainy Sunday morning in 2016, and I've decided to write a book. It has been 12 years since my first deployment and five years since my last, but recently finding my daily journal I kept in Iraq makes it feel like yesterday. After 28 years of military service, as an infantryman and an attorney, I retired as an Air Force JAG in March 2015.[1] Although I avoid watching certain movies and news reports that show the houses, towns, and people in rural parts of the Middle East because of the stress it causes me, I have found it somewhat entertaining to tell stories of my exploits when people ask. I have now decided to share these funny and interesting stories of a JAG at war! It is almost funny to say "attorney" and "war" in the same sentence.

Without boring you with the details of how I got there, *there* being serving in the military, I will provide you with a backdrop of my senior year in high school. I was 17 years old and wanted to do something "different." It would not take much for something to be different to me. You see, living my entire life up to that point in a town of 5,000 people in Southeast Arkansas, just about anything outside of my hometown would be considered different to me. I wanted to travel, see the world,

---

[1] The term JAG stands for Judge Advocate General. They are licensed attorneys who serve primarily as legal advisors to the command to which they are assigned. Their advice may cover a wide range of issues dealing with administrative law, government contracting, civilian and military personnel law, law of war and international relations, and environmental law, etc. They also serve as prosecutors for the military when conducting courts-martial. Most apply for a competitive position after graduating from law school where the selection rate is approximately 7–10%.

have an adventure; but I also wanted to become an attorney. In the mind of a 17-year-old, those ideas seemed to fit together logically much better than looking back at that idea 30 years later. I had dreams of becoming a military intelligence officer. I liked knowing secrets. Perhaps I had always enjoyed secrets. That's why I enjoyed watching and performing magic tricks and fooling my older sisters with the "little brother magic shows." I had a friend whose father had been a military intelligence officer; his father was quiet, didn't talk unless you asked him something, and then only a few words. He was kind of mysterious to me. Although I was just the opposite, talking until someone told me to stop talking (my parents must have been saints to let me talk nonstop), I figured I could still make it work.

Ready to take on the world at 17 with just months before graduating from high school, I drove to a nearby town about 20 miles away to find a military recruiter. This was 1987 and my hometown didn't even have a Walmart, much less a military recruiting office. I walked in the… Wait a minute. I think I should let you know that I didn't just wake up and decide to join the military.

My interest in military service was ignited when I saw the movie *An Officer and a Gentleman*. You know, with Debra Winger and Richard Gere. The character played by Richard Gere had no other options in life except to join the Navy and try to become a Navy pilot. He entered Navy flight school and was given a hard time by his drill sergeant. Although the character's last name was Mayo, he was affectionately called Mayonnaise by his drill sergeant. During the training, the drill sergeant picked on him more than anyone else and tried to make him quit. In the end, Mayo graduates and gets the girl. I said, "That is the life for me." But, not as a pilot, as a lawyer! This was before the famous quote from the movie *A Few Good Men*—"You can't handle the truth!"

I mailed a request, yes pre-internet and email, circa 1985, to the U.S. Naval Academy and requested information and an application. In the information book, listed as one of the qualifications for candidates was to be able to float in the water for at least 20 minutes. So, in the summer, I went to the member's only pool we had in my hometown to practice floating. As my friends and I jumped off the diving boards, splashed the girls, and had chicken fights, I'd sneak away and secretly tried to stay afloat for 20 minutes without my friends seeing what I was doing or thinking I was drowning. How embarrassing it would have been to see the lifeguards sitting up on those high perches actually stop flirting with the girls and jump in the water to save me when all I was doing was trying to stay afloat in four feet of water! Yes, me, the boy whose mother made him start taking swimming lessons at three years old because *she* could not swim.

To be accepted into the U.S. Naval Academy, it required a recommendation from a U.S. Senator. My dad set up a meeting with Senator David Pryor. He was nice, recommended I read the book *Catcher in the Rye*, and asked me several questions. Unfortunately, my grades in high school were not as high as needed to receive a recommendation. I would not be going to the academy, but I was able to float for 20 minutes if that skill were ever needed!

Okay, back to the recruiter's office. He was a nice Army sergeant, very friendly. Now 30 years later, I know why he was so friendly. I told him I wanted to have an adventure and thought military intelligence was the way for me. He showed me some videos of different military jobs to make sure that was the one I wanted. Yep, that is the only one I wanted. I told him I did not want a long-term commitment. I even had trouble with that with my girlfriend, who I liked a lot more than I imagined I would the Army. The recruiter, always polite and reassuring, told me that I could join the Army with only a two-year contract and become a military intelligence soldier! And then, was on my way. I figured I would go to college at night as my father did for four years in the Army. But I figured I would not do anything as cool as my dad, such as make false teeth for my grandfather! My dad had joined the Army after running out of college money, so he did a short stint in the Army to go to college at night and earn money to complete his college degree after leaving the Army. I was going to do it differently. I would go to the Army first.

My mom, always supportive, would have to sign the paperwork to allow me to join at age 17. Anything to support her baby son, the only boy in the family. I'm not sure if she even told my dad. My recruiter told me to go to Little Rock, about 75 miles away, and go through a physical exam at the Military Entrance Processing Station (MEPS). The Army paid for my hotel the night before and gave me coupons for free meals at the restaurant. I felt as though I was being treated like I was the number one soldier, and I had not even signed a contract!

Early the next morning, like before-daylight-can-strike-your-eyes early, the bus came to the hotel to pick us up, a group of wannabe soldiers. It dropped us off at the MEPS station to begin the process that takes several hours. After walking like a duck in my underwear (I'm still not sure what medical condition it was supposed to disclose), bench pressing 50 lbs. or so, and having the doctors tell me nothing was wrong with my boy parts, I finally made it to the "man at a computer." Each of us who made it through the physical exam would sit down with the man at the computer, one at a time. He decided the job you would have in the military by punching a few keys on his keyboard. He asked me what I wanted to do in the Army.

I proudly said, "Military intelligence."

He said, "How long do you want to enlist?"

I said, "Two years," proudly and eagerly awaited a few clicks of the computer keys and be on my way to an adventure outside my small Southeast Arkansas town.

Instead, I got, "Sorry son, you cannot 'go' military intelligence with a two-year commitment." I was shocked, I figured this is where they try to get you to "buy" more than you wanted, just like a car salesman, or they had certain career fields they were trying to fill. I explained that my recruiter said I could go into military intelligence with a two-year contract. The soldier just shook his head and said no.

I said, "Then let's call the recruiter."

Now, it was the soldier who was saying, "What?" as if no one had ever questioned him. The soldier said I could become a soldier in the supply section of the Army with a two-year commitment.

I responded, "Are you crazy? If I wanted to stock shelves, I would have gotten a job at the local Mad Butcher or Piggly Wiggly grocery store." What kind of secrets would I learn in a supply store? The soldier agreed to call my recruiter and explain the situation. The recruiter apologized and said he must have made a mistake. I believe the recruiter knew all along that I could not go into military intelligence with a two-year contract but had hoped I would be pressured to sign up for a longer time or a different job. How many 17-year-old kids would have succumbed to the pressure of an Army sergeant at a computer? Not me. I told the soldier and the recruiter that I was leaving. The soldier looked stunned, but I knew, at least the future lawyer in me thought I knew, that I was not obligated to join the Army because I had not signed any contract. I caught a taxi back to the hotel, got in my car, and went home.

A few months later, some friends of mine in high school were talking about joining the National Guard. We had an armory in our small town, but I had no idea what they did there, other than host dances for kids now and again. We discussed how it would be fun for us to all go away to college and come back once a month to visit our families and go to the armory for weekend drills. I learned the pay was about $170 for a weekend. Wow! That is a lot to an 18-year-old kid who had never really worked (of course, this was 1987). I could use that money for a good time at college without feeling guilty about asking my parents for money to party. I also learned the Army National Guard would pay some of my college loans back. Now, that is a good idea. I had to figure out what career field was available in the armory in town. Of all things… infantry. Oh, man! Let me take a few seconds to describe myself physically. I was an 18- year-old kid, 5'7" tall, and 110 lbs. Maybe 115 with all my clothes on and some loose change in my pockets. Okay, let's do this. What 18-year-old kid doesn't think he can do anything anyway?

Once again, I find myself at the same hotel in Little Rock. The free meals did not sound as exciting this time, but much more exciting than having to spend hours walking like a duck in my underwear with a bunch of strange guys and then having my junk inspected again by a doctor who had one eye that wandered around its socket. I thought I would do even better walking like a duck since I would be the experienced one in the group. What an award that would have been, "Best underwear duckwalking contestant."

I made it through the exam, signed the contract to be an infantryman, and was on my way to a military career. Well, not exactly. I was only conditionally approved. I had to go back to MEPS in Little Rock in a couple of weeks to get re-weighed because they said I was too skinny. I only weighed 113 and that was not enough. After going home, drinking milkshakes, and eating as much as I could, I returned to the MEPS station, weighed again, and weighed enough to be trained to be shot at. Without boring you with the eight years I spent in the National Guard while attending college and law school, I will say a few good things about my experience. Other than having to come back earlier than my classmates from my high school senior trip to Florida in order to go to basic training, and other than having to practice running while my friends laid around the beach, my stint in the National Guard was very beneficial. For example, attending law school five hours away from the armory, allowed my wife to drive me once a month to the weekend drill while I sat in the passenger seat studying for law school for about 10 hours! The infantry training would also come in handy when I found myself, as an attorney, in charge of an office of 11 officers and enlisted members in the middle of Iraq nine years later.

My military service continued after graduating from law school. Although I had hopes of becoming a small-town lawyer who joined the large church and country club in some town, the military came knocking at my door again. In the third year of law school, various law firms come to campus to interview future lawyers for jobs. As I was coming out of an interview with a law firm that did not go so well and would not result in me getting that $26K/year job as a new associate, I saw an Air Force officer in the hallway of the law school building. There is always a certain bond and friendliness amongst military members. I asked him what the Air Force was doing at a law school. He explained the Air Force was hiring attorneys called JAGs. JAGs? I know about them. My parents watched that television show *JAG* every week. The one where the Navy JAG named "Harm" gets to fly planes, defuse bombs, and has these gorgeous paralegals. The Air Force JAG explained that the salary was almost twice as much as the firms were paying new law associates in Arkansas. In addition, there was travel, and a chance to litigate real cases during my first weeks on the job! I was excited to apply. I had to submit a writing sample, undergo a background check, and have an interview with a real JAG who would write a recommendation (good or bad) to the Air Force board who selects the top 10% of the applicants. I know, I was in the Army National Guard, but I had no qualms about switching to the Air Force. Besides, the Air

Force's blue uniform would match my eyes, and I had been told if you wanted a metal desk to join the Army and if you wanted a wooden desk, then join the Air Force. I also knew from experience that the Army slept in tents (at least I had for eight years) and I had been told the Air Force slept at the Holiday Inn.

To cut to the chase, as it is no secret, I was selected to become a JAG. Off to Montgomery, Alabama for two weeks of officer training with the preachers; I know, interesting training group, learning to march and wear our uniforms. Unlike the Army experience where you arrived at basic training on a bus and were immediately chased off the bus by drill sergeants, the Air Force mailed me documents to sign to be officially a 1st lieutenant in the Air Force. After returning the documents, the Air Force told me to find my way to Montgomery, Alabama on a certain date for training. After the two-week officer training with the new chaplains and attorneys, I was told to go across town and start JAG school. Again, unlike my Army experience, the Air Force accommodations included individual rooms like a hotel suite; it was the Air Force version of a Marriot. It had a queen-size bed, table, chairs, refrigerator, private bathroom (of course), a large TV, and a nice view of the military base. Oh! And let's not forget the daily maid service to our rooms! I could not believe the huge difference in my experience from being the lowest enlisted grade in the Army to the second-lowest officer grade in the Air Force.

My nine weeks of the Air Force version of law school included a flight to Washington D.C. to visit the Pentagon and the Air Force Court of Criminal Appeals and a bus ride down to the panhandle of Florida to visit the Air Force Special Operations folks. After passing my examinations and graduating from the Air Force JAG School, I was told to find my way to my first assignment in Shreveport, Louisiana. Yes, I asked for that assignment. It was only a couple of hours from home. I told you that it does not take much for a small-town boy to call something an adventure. The rest of my career included several of the southern states I chose, such as Georgia, Mississippi, Oklahoma, and Texas. There were a couple of stray assignments up north to Massachusetts and Washington D.C., and of course, Iraq and Afghanistan.

LEAVING ON A JET PLANE

In 2004, in my ninth year as a JAG, I was deployed to Iraq. It would be the first of two deployments. While in Iraq, I kept a journal to capture interesting events. I wanted to be able to share with my family and my friends what I should not and could not share with them while I was gone because it would have been unfair to make them worry about me.

Ten years after returning from my deployment to the infamous prison in Abu Ghraib, Iraq, I found my journal. The information below is mostly in journal format and records my experiences. I have gone back and added some comments to the journal entries to give it more depth. It was another great adventure!

The theme of the journal and the adventure itself is how to keep a smile and a positive attitude in a difficult situation. There are humorous parts, sad parts, and great stories about bullets, bathrooms, and bad guys, so buckle up!

October 5, 2004. Tuesday

My war story begins in 2004 at Altus Air Force Base in Southwest Oklahoma, where I was stationed. At my kids' bedtime on October 5, 2004, I said goodbye to my 13-year-old daughter Bianca and six-year-old son Tripp. As I hugged my son, I could not help from crying because I knew he didn't fully understand where I was going and the possibility that I may not be able to return. I was afraid that if I did not return, he may forget me or, worse, think I did not want to return. My daughter, being a young teenager, was old enough to comprehend the situation and put on a brave face.

October 6, 2004. Wednesday

I kissed my wife goodbye and got in a taxi on October 6, 2004, at 4:30 am to go to war. I had already made peace with myself, written goodbye letters to my wife and kids, in case I did not come back, and accepted the fact that the Air Force creed I had been saying for the last nine years, "service before self" comes down to this very moment.

My paralegal and I traveled two hours by taxi from Altus AFB, Oklahoma to Oklahoma City. We then caught a commercial plane to Dallas. I have to admit, it was kind of strange checking our bags in at the airline counter, along with a couple of machine guns. Yep, post-911, we put our machine guns and pistols in a plastic gun case, locked it with mini-locks, and then turned them over to the airline ticket counter like I was checking my shaving cream and underwear. We flew from Oklahoma City to Dallas to Baltimore then to Frankfurt, Germany to Qatar, which is a small country on the Persian Gulf that serves as a stationing depot. The last stop before the combat zone to Iraq is Qatar. It was non-stop traveling for 32 hours. We were lucky enough to be able to get off the plane in Frankfurt to stretch our legs, but we had to stay in a little hallway inside the airport terminal away from the public. Luckily, they did have a small store where we could buy drinks and snacks, and even souvenirs. I bought a refrigerator magnet at the store on my way to war! I still have it! I always liked collecting magnets from all my travels, even though my wife won't allow magnets on the refrigerator. She says something about it looking tacky, which I will never understand.

October 8, 2004. Friday

We arrived in the little country of Qatar at 2:30 am local time on a Friday, which was 6 pm Thursday back home. I'm never sure how to pronounce the name of Qatar. Some say Key-Tar, some say Kay-Tar, and some say KeTar. No matter how you say it, it held the first bed I had seen in a day and a half. I fell asleep at 4:30 am local time, but I awoke at 6:45 am local time. It must have been the noise in the room of 100+ guys sleeping on squeaky metal bunk beds. My excitement was high. I was in a safe country that served as a pit stop for soldiers on their way to Iraq. I wanted to walk around the base to see what a foreign country in the Middle East looked like. After my shower, I made it to a concrete patio about 40 yards squared. It had a nice roof to block the unstoppable sun and it stood awaiting the time the sun would reach its peak. At one end of the patio was a little trailer or building. It's hard to say what exactly it was. Most of the structures there were not permanent, so even buildings look temporary and somewhat of a hybrid between prefabricated metal storage sheds and trailers. I saw people going through the line to get into the building. One thing you learn on deployment is to look and listen to find out what is going on around you. There is no tour guide. There is no one holding your hand or even telling you how to find food or shelter. You have to figure it out yourself. Deploying as a JAG means it's just you. No commander or sergeant is giving you orders of where to go, what to do next, or what to expect. Walking toward the line, I felt like I was in slow motion. Perhaps this is what jet lag feels like. Or, perhaps the lack of sleep has made me intoxicated. Or, it could have been the drop in the initial adrenaline I had felt when I woke up in a strange country.

As I got in line, I listened to others talking so I could learn why we were in line. It is always good to figure that out quickly. Luckily, it was a line to get a "beer card." Yep, that's right. In Qatar, we were allowed to purchase two beers every 24 hours. They punched your card each time you got a beer so they can track how many you have purchased. Way too early to drink, besides I already had a buzz created by my long journey, that had not even really started. I figured I would get a beer card as another souvenir, even if I did not use it. Afterwards, I decided to walk around the base because I had heard other people saying the plane to Iraq would not be leaving for a few hours. Qatar has a swimming pool and a nice dining facility. I thought that if the place where I am going is like this, then I would have it made. Unfortunately, or fortunately, at that time, I had no idea that the place I was headed was the opposite of this oasis. As I walked around, I found the place welcoming. Military members take care of each other. Even pickup trucks who passed you walking on the gravel and sandy roads that crisscrossed the base would ask if you wanted a ride. You have to imagine Kansas with sand instead of fields of grass. The buildings were spread out and you could walk a long way just to learn you had walked the wrong direction. They had buses that could take you around the base, but if you can avoid sitting in the hot sun with no shade waiting on a bus then it's best to take up the offer of a ride.

COMING IN, HOT OR NOT

At about 11 am, it was time to leave this place and enter the "real" war zone. Without even having a chance to get my beer card punched, I boarded a C130 with approximately 30 other people. It was going to be an uncomfortable ride. We each had three or four duffel bags full of gear and uniforms to last four–six months; some had put on their body armor and taken their machine guns out of their gun cases and strapped their 9mm pistols to their waist. I loaded up with just my helmet on and my weapons safely secured behind three mini-locks in a gun case. I started thinking, *Hey, I don't have a chance. How am I going to land in a war zone with luggage? I won't be able to protect myself.* Too late! The plane is starting to taxi down the runway. For those not familiar with a C130, it isn't like a commercial jet I had just spent nearly two days on. No, this is a propeller plane, made to take off and land on short runways made of dirt! Off we go. Earplugs in, helmet on, and an "oh, sh!t" look on my face. I knew from my years in the Infantry that when the plane lands it could be a hot landing zone, so you have to come out ready to shoot!

About two and a half hours later I feel the plane making circles in the air. Not the kind the commercial planes do when circling an airport to wait their turn to land. No, this was a corkscrew-type circling. I learned later that the C130 flew above the Baghdad International Airport (BIAP) and then started doing tight circles to land. This was to prevent having to fly low over the land for a long period of time and getting shot down by a missile. I started realizing that wearing body armor and carrying a weapon would have been good ideas since the pilots were taking these landing precautions due to threats.

Upon landing, we taxied to the opposite side of the airport away from the main terminal. The plane stopped near an area with tents set up along the runway. We were hurried off the plane and shuffled to a specific area to wait for our duffel bags to be unloaded (and my case containing my weapons). Now that I made it to Baghdad, I had no way of knowing if anyone was going to pick me up. Did anyone even know I was there? After ensuring my green bags had been unloaded along with hundreds of other green bags—mine were easy to spot with bright pink ribbons to make them stand out in the sea of green bags—I went to look for a phone. One nice thing is we did not have to worry about anyone walking off with our bags because everyone already had their own bags that they did not want to carry much less carrying anyone else's.

I found a phone in one of the tents. I had carried a binder with my military orders, documents to enter the country, and a phone number of the legal office in Baghdad located on Camp Victory, where I would be assigned. I did not know it at the time, but Camp Victory was inside the same perimeter as BIAP. After calling the legal office and being told someone was on their way to pick us up, I went back to my bags. As soon as I sat down, sure enough, Major Stoup, a fellow Air Force JAG arrived to give us a lift. He looked clean and refreshed with no body armor or helmet. He was, however, wearing a handgun on his belt. We threw our bags into the back of his SUV, then I stopped to grab my weapons and body armor out of my bags. I wanted to make sure I had them ready to go before I ventured any further. Major Stoup assured me the body armor and weapons were not necessary where we were going. I did not know this guy, nor did I know if he was some John

Wayne type. Not me, I am from a small town in Southeast Arkansas, and wearing body armor and weapons seems like a common-sense thing to do in Baghdad!

I decided to trust him that I did not need protection just traveling a few miles inside the perimeter. I figured the worst-case scenario; I could stand behind him when the shooting starts or use his weapon if he crumbles. Luckily, this did not happen, but thinking ahead is going to be key to surviving this journey. We traveled about 10 miles down dirt/sandy roads and stopped in an area called Camp Victory. We parked outside one of Saddam Hussein's palaces sitting on the lake. I believe it was called his summer palace. It had been turned into some type of embassy for us. Inside was very impressive. It was my first visit to a palace, and it was as fancy as I could have imagined. It was a different world inside the palace compared to what I would see anywhere else in this country.

The palace walls were all shiny with gold plated objects, marble floors, and huge staircases. It even had a swimming pool in the back! I started thinking this deployment gig may not be too bad. First Qatar with a beer card, now a palace! How bad can this be? Of course, little did I know, the place I would spend my deployment could not be any more different than the palace. After visiting an office inside for some business Major Stoup had to take care of so he could redeploy back home, we got back into the SUV and drove a quarter way around the lake. There was a building across the street from the lake that housed the legal office. Inside, I would learn my fate of where I would be working for the next four months.

<u>ORDERED TO PRISON</u>

As we stood there being stared at by the old-timers, my paralegal from home was told his assignment first. He will be going to the embassy across town. It is another one of Saddam's old palaces. Alright! I must be going to a place equally as nice, right? Nope, not even close. I would be assigned as the officer in charge, in a place in the opposite direction, about 15 miles away from Baghdad. A place the whole world had been introduced to and hated… Abu Ghraib.

It was now October 2004, and it had only been a few months since the television news reports were covering Abu Ghraib non-stop. There had been some soldiers there that were mistreating the Iraqi prisoners. The soldiers were court-martialed, but people in Iraq were still livid. The Iraqis did not even like the place when Saddam was in power because he used it as a place for torture. I was going to the most hated place in the country. The place all Americans probably believed is where all military folks must be mistreating prisoners. A place that caused the locals to despise us even more. Okay, Abu Ghraib, again with the names. Is it pronounced Gray-b or Grawwb? Who knows? I was more concerned with how it looked. The news reports never really showed the whole base, or did they? I couldn't remember. Surely it will contain marble floors or gold-plated toilets like the palaces, right? I will know soon enough. But first, we have to make some stops for meetings in the "red zone."

October 9, 2004. Saturday

The red zone is not a nice place. Red as in stop or danger, which is opposite of green, where the intersection is safe and you can walk freely. The palaces were in the green zone, but Abu Ghraib was in the red zone. Green zones are secured areas. Red zones are unsecured. The next morning began like a typical military day. Up at 6 am, breakfast at 7 am, then put on the body armor, get the weapons out of the plastic case this time, lock and load, and ready to convoy out. However, my deployment boss, Army Colonel John Phelps, asked me to do something before I went. On the way out of the dining hall after breakfast, he handed me a small box of cereal and told me to put it in my pocket for later. When we arrived back at the legal office, instead of loading up on the convoy, Colonel Phelps told me to follow him across the street to the lake on which Saddam's summer palace sat. Colonel Phelps instructed me to take out the box of cereal and throw some in the lake. I did as I was told. As soon as the cereal hit the water, carps and eels swam to the surface and ate the cereal. Saddam supposedly had these carps flown in from Japan and China, but who knows. You hear a lot of things over here. After enjoying the sight, we hurried across the street, loaded up the trucks of the convoy, and prepared to make our journey into the danger zone. I was hoping that feeding the fish experience was not Colonel Phelps' way of saying good luck and goodbye. I wondered how many other JAGs he had taken to feed the fish that did not make it back.

<u>OUTSIDE THE WIRE</u>

My first trip outside the "wire" is to a hotel where most journalists stay. A convoy of four trucks with a .50 caliber weapon on top of two of them and bulletproof armor on the sides pulled up outside our office. Their job was to escort a military intelligence officer, a security forces officer (Air Force policeman), and three attorneys to the meeting location in the red zone and ensure we arrive unharmed. The first and last trucks have the .50 caliber rifles on top. The two middle trucks only have bulletproof armor. I chose my seat carefully because it could decide my fate on these dangerous roads ahead. I rode in the backseat of the second truck behind the passenger. I figured following behind the first armored truck would be like the running back in football following behind the right guard. I had no rhyme or reason for my opinion, just good ole country logic.

    The trip would take about 30 minutes. There is no such thing as being offended for being tailgated out here. The four trucks traveled close together in what is called a stack formation. We drove fast and never stopped. Now, think about that for a minute. Baghdad is not a small town. It has over 25 million people and most seem to be on its crowded roads. We never stopped in bumper to bumper traffic! We finally make it to the outside of the hotel. We pull up to the secured gate to get waved inside the safe perimeter walls of the hotel. However, the poor enlisted soldier with three stripes on his sleeve says we cannot enter. The balls to tell armored trucks with colonels they cannot go somewhere. The Army colonel in our truck cursed at the poor soldier to let us in, but the soldier holds tight saying we are not on the list. The list? What list? We are in Army trucks, with Army people with Army uniforms. Okay, I was the one Air Force guy. What other evidence do you need to have to know we are in the U.S. military? If you can hear my voice, you would know it is South Arkansas, not South Baghdad. Nevertheless, the poor young soldier follows his orders and refuses to let us enter because our names are not on the paper he has in the middle of a war zone! We back up all four trucks and turn around to keep from blocking the entrance. Our Army colonel passenger now has to leave the safety of the armored vehicle, walk across the parking lot, and go inside a building to force them to let us inside the gates. It works. We finally get to park the trucks inside the perimeter. It is not just a matter of not wanting to walk across the parking lot due to the heat or a sniper. There is a certain danger of leaving vehicles in the parking lot, which you will hear about later.

Inside one of the meeting rooms, there is a Combined Review and Release Board (CRRB) taking place. Some people call it the *Confined* Review and Release Board. The people in my convoy are the board members and they do exactly what the name of the board says. The three to four officers assigned will review case files of Iraqi prisoners and foreign fighters who have been caught and decide which ones should be released and which ones should remain detained. These are fighters who have been captured and now a decision has to be made as to what to do with them. Can we let them go and not worry about them trying to kill our troops again? Do we have enough evidence to believe they were trying to harm us? These meetings are also referred to as detainee hearings. It is similar to the preliminary hearings we hear about in Guantanamo Bay or "GITMO" in Cuba. I would soon learn that I would be one of the cogs in the machine of this process.

If the person is a threat, we keep them locked up. If we believe they committed a crime under Iraqi law, then we send them to the Iraqi prosecutor to be tried in the Central Criminal Court of Iraq. It may not sound fair that only U.S. soldiers are deciding if Iraqis are a threat. Therefore, the board also has four to six Iraqi members assigned. Two are from the Iraqi Department of the Interior, two are from the Iraqi Department of Justice, and two are from the Iraqi Department of Human Rights. During that one day, we discussed 150 cases. The Iraqi members usually recognize the names of the detainees or the neighborhood where the detainee was captured. It takes a majority of the votes to keep the person detained. It is not a criminal trial, so the burden is not that high. Often, there is only a witness statement or two from the soldiers who captured the person. I learned three new Arabic words that day. There is no telling if I am spelling them correctly, so assume I am not. The first word is "Kafala," which means to release with a guarantor (someone who promises the detainee will not commit a crime), "Habaas" means to intern (keep them locked up), and the third one is "Efraj," which means an unconditional release of the detainee.

I guess to give you a more accurate vision of the "conference room" in a hotel where the board met, I should describe it better. The room was on the second or third floor and had no windows. On two sides of the room, plastic served as walls because a bomb had taken part of the walls out. The walls also contained many bullet holes. [Looking through the old news, I believe the name of the hotel was Hotel al-Rasheed. CNN of course covered the whole story when it happened in October 2003 when rockets attacked and killed several Americans. Reports said that attackers dropped off a trailer containing a rocket launcher disguised as a generator that started firing rockets at the hotel. A month prior, the hotel was attacked by an RPG].

After a day of watching the discussions that determined people's fate, I traveled across Baghdad to the embassy/palace where my paralegal was working. His workspace was magnificent. It was what you would imagine in a beautiful palace. He too was a cog in the machine. His office would work on the cases that had been forwarded to the Iraqi prosecutors from the CRRB.

That night, I was setting up my gear to sleep in a tent not far from the embassy/palace instead of traveling back to Camp Victory. One of the Army paralegals assigned to the office was helping me get my gear. We walked outside to get my four duffel bags off the truck in the convoy. That is when it happened. It was Saturday at 8:12 pm. Boom! As soon as I walked outside, a mortar exploded about 150 yards to our front left. The Army paralegal and I immediately ran back inside the tent. It seemed like the obvious thing to do. You know, take cover "inside." But, looking back it is obvious a few millimeters of fabric would not have provided any protection.

We could see through the doorway of the tent that smoke from the explosion was rising. We waited about a minute then proceeded outside again. We retrieved my bags and set up the beds inside the tent, which held about 20 cots. Within a few minutes of setting up, the word came down that people could not sleep in the tent because it was unsafe. I took my bags and threw them back into the truck where I was driven to a warehouse closer to the embassy/palace. We still would not be inside the fence line of the embassy though. We had to pass outside the brick and mortar perimeter walls of the embassy to get to the warehouse. There were soldiers from Nepal that guarded the opening in the wall that led to the outside world where the warehouse was located. Rumors had it that Nepalese soldiers were tough as nails. They sure looked it. Inside the warehouse were hundreds of wooden beds. It was about 30 beds wide and about 10 beds deep. It was just a huge warehouse full of beds. It was loud but it had air conditioning! It is amazing how physically exhausting it can be to keep your mind and body on alert all the time.

After locating some empty bunks and dropping some of our gear off, I took off my boots and lay on my bunk to read a binder full of information about my new assignment in this horrible place I had yet to visit. As people from the tents started piling into the warehouse, so did the stories. One military policeman who had arrived a few days before me exclaimed that the day after he moved out of the tents, a mortar landed on them. That was his close call. I would soon have mine. In my first two days in the war, I had visited two palaces and survived my first mortar attack. Of course, it gives no comfort to know that "they" say that you never hear the mortar that gets you. So far, I have survived. But my war is just beginning. By the way, today was my wife's birthday and I did not have an opportunity to call home.

October 10, 2004. Sunday

The next morning, I awoke to get ready and go to the legal office inside the palace. I was somewhat surprised, still being new to a combat zone, that there was no water in the "watersheds." The watersheds are just as they sound. They are little metal sheds about the size of a storage shed you might have at home in your backyard. Inside the watersheds were several small showers and a few sinks. Quickly learning to improvise, adapt, and overcome, I went to the swimming pool in the back of the palace. I found a changing room/bathhouse beside the pool. It had a small shower and sink, so I locked the door and took a shower, and dressed for day two in the war zone.

While meeting with people in the upstairs office, I heard stories about how the toilets are made of gold. Of course, I have to go to the bathroom to check it out. Sure enough, inside the palace, the sinks and toilets had gold plated trims. How many people can say they set upon a real gold "throne?" I can!

HEADING TO COURT

In the office, we discussed our trip to the Central Criminal Court of Iraq (CCCI) that we had to make that day. That is where the detainees are prosecuted after the Combined Review and Release Board (CRRB) had reviewed their case and referred them to the Iraqi prosecutor. The detainees are tried by Iraqi prosecutors and the cases are decided by Iraqi judges. Before the trip, we are briefed that there will be three Toyota Land Cruisers which have been armored, but with no gun mounts. You cannot tell it is bulletproof except for the glass. I decided to ride in the second vehicle again. I rode with the translator while two young security forces guys, who were about 20 years old, occupied the front seats. We put on our body armor, locked and loaded our weapons, and prepared for the 15-minute drive across Baghdad. It was about 9 am and traffic on the Baghdad streets was busy. True to form, we travelled through heavy traffic but never stopped. We zig-zagged around traffic and even hit 100 kph on some stretches. We blew the horn to make the cars around us move. The convoy drivers must constantly maneuver to prohibit cars from getting in between the trucks in the convoy. It was pretty scary. Our trucks get bumper-to-bumper but never stop! It was absolutely amazing. There were several barricades set up by armed Iraqis and U.S. troops. We go through many of them and we cut across the medians in the roads several times and even do U-turns all to ensure no one can get a good shot at us. Finally, we reached the courthouse.

The translator, Navy JAG, and two paralegals and I get out of the vehicles that have pulled up near the front doors. The four security forces members surround us in a diamond formation and escort us up the walkway and into the courthouse. Inside, Iraqi civilians are walking around conducting their everyday business. Iraqi police have weapons but are not checking any visitors who enter. That means anyone inside can be armed, and I don't mean just the good guys. Three of our escorts take positions in different areas of the courthouse. They stand on the second story balcony where they can see downstairs and upstairs. The other escort walks us to one of the rooms that connect to a courtroom. We drop our gear, long rifles, body armor, but keep our M9s on our hips. You never want to be naked when things go bad. We enter a large room where 10 Army military policemen (MP) are guarding three Iraqi detainees who are dressed in yellow jumpsuits and sitting in chairs facing the wall. The detainees are about 30 feet from each other and about 60 feet from the MPs who are sitting at a table playing cards. Some of the MPs get up and escort the first Iraqi detainee into the adjoining courtroom. One MP stays in the courtroom with the detainee. The inside of the courtroom looks mostly like one you would see in the U.S. But there are some differences. For example, instead of one judge, three Iraqi judges are sitting at a bench in the front of the courtroom, one Iraqi prosecutor at a podium on the left side, and one Iraqi defense attorney at a podium on the right side. There is one major difference between an Iraqi courtroom and a U.S. courtroom. In Iraq, the detainee/defendant stands in a cage beside the defense attorney. Yes, standing! Yes, in a cage!

The first detainee entered the cage. He was apparently caught with one mortar and one RPG in his car. The primary evidence was a witness statement from a U.S. soldier. The witness statement is read out loud by the prosecutor. The defendant says he doesn't know anything about the weapons. I keep my eyes peeled and scan the room, not knowing if anyone there is a "bad" guy or has a weapon. I heard loud statements in Arabic coming from the right side of the room. An Iraqi policeman was standing in the aisle telling everyone to get out of the room! Everyone stood up and walked to the back of the room and out the door into the hallway. I look around and notice even the detainee was brought out too. I see our MPs still spread out scanning the crowds in the courthouse. The MP who was with us in the courtroom makes the detainee face the wall outside in the hallway. In less than one minute, the Iraqi policeman tells us to go back inside the courtroom. Before everyone was able to sit down, one of the Iraqi judges, who stayed in the courtroom, announces "guilty" and sentences the defendant to two years in prison and has him escorted out. I would guess the whole ordeal took about 15 minutes and it was not as if the defendant had pled guilty. Now, that is judicial efficiency!

The second detainee was then escorted into the courtroom by one of the MPs and placed in his cage beside his Iraqi defense attorney.

This detainee had a more interesting story. He was detained for shooting at coalition forces with an AK 47 when they kicked in his front door at 3:30 in the morning. When the shooting started, the coalition forces threw a hand grenade into the house and injured the detainee's leg. The detainee said he thought the coalition forces were his neighbors who he had been fighting with. So, that is how they handle disputes with neighbors in Baghdad. Forget about toilet papering a tree or egging a car…just pick up an AK 47 and start shooting! Again, the Iraqi police tell everyone to leave the courtroom. About one minute later, they tell everyone to get back inside. Before we all sit down, one of the judges announces "guilty" and "one year in jail."

During my introduction to Iraqi justice, I did not say a word. I just sat there with my hand on my M9 pistol and watched. After the "trial," we walked to the judges' bench and were introduced to the top Iraqi judge. He was kind and wished us all peace. That is when I noticed another big difference between Iraqi court procedures and the U.S., I saw the court reporter taking the transcript by hand. She handwrote everything that was said on carbon copy paper. She wore a scarf on her hair and gave our female Iraqi translator a nasty look because she was not wearing a scarf over her hair. I guess women everywhere judge each other's appearances. While wrapping up our observation and meeting at the courthouse that day, we heard several mortars explode. The court did not halt and no one took any action. People just continued as normal, except for us. We grabbed our gear and the MPs formed a diamond around us and escorted us to the convoy quickly. I imagine no visit to the courthouse is fun for non-attorneys, but this trip was unpleasant for everyone. Amongst the stress, it was calming to see our brave MPs standing in the hallway upstairs and at the doors to ensure us attorneys and paralegals were safe.

The bathroom in the courthouse was an experience all by itself. After visiting it, you tell yourself you will never drink coffee again before going to the courthouse.

Our convoy back to the embassy was uneventful. Shortly after arriving, it was time for me to relocate. I had seen the second and third steps in the detainee hearing process, which was intended to give me the much-needed foundation as I head to my assignment to lead the first step in the process. I was told to get on the Rhino to travel back to BIAP and Camp Victory, where the summer palace and legal office is on the lake and both of Saddam's son's palaces, or what is left of them, sit crumbled from bombings. Now, the Rhino I was riding is not the animal type. It is an armored RV type vehicle. It was a huge target for the bad guys, but the outside steel plates hopefully would prevent their attack. Luckily, to deter the bad guys from attacking the convoy of two

Rhinos, an armored truck with a .50 caliber machine gun on top and a white suburban full of U.S. civilian fighters (contracted by the U.S. government) led the Rhinos while an identical set of an armored truck and white suburban followed. You can't help but feel a little helpless inside a Rhino. A mortar or an RPG could easily find its mark on the side of the Rhino. Our instructions were to stay inside if we were attacked and let the four trucks take care of any problems. Luckily, we made the 45-minute drive across Baghdad without any problems. Of course, problems "move" out of the way when you see the six-vehicle convoy that never stops!

Once back at BIAP, my paralegal from home was there to meet me just like Major Stoup had done just a couple of days earlier on my first day. We loaded our truck and traveled inside the perimeter back to Camp Victory, which is the formal name of the area which contains the palace on the lake. Even as we traveled within the relatively safe area, we could hear mortars explode. There was this large blimp, like a smaller Goodyear blimp that flew above the camp. Its purpose was to provide a bird's eye view of a 13-mile radius and help zero in on the location from which these mortars were fired. Once the location is detected, helicopters get there in less than two minutes. At least that is how people explained it to us. There was an issue with one helicopter that clipped the wire to the blimp and the blimp had to be shot down and destroyed to keep it out of enemy hands. Around suppertime, mortars hit about every 10 minutes for about an hour. The rest of the time they hit about once every 45 minutes. It sounds like really close episodes of claps of thunder. Some shake the ground or building you're in.

Tomorrow, I head to my new home for the next four months…Abu Ghraib. All I have heard was it is a prison, it gets mortared all the time, there is no running water and no toilets. I also heard Iraqis tried to charge the prison two weeks ago. Sounds interesting! Oh, yea, it has been on the news for U.S. soldiers torturing Iraqi prisoners, so it is not a popular place to be.

PART II

TIME IN PRISON

HEADING TO PRISON

October 11, 2004. Monday

I woke up for the last time in a relatively safe place at Camp Victory. I showered, packed my gear, and went to the legal office by the lake. After sitting around until 2:30 pm, it was time to load the truck and go meet the convoy of 28 trucks that will make the 15-mile trip to Abu Ghraib. After a co-worker dropped my bags and me off at the edge of the camp near a gate where the convoy was meeting, I walked around to find a seat in one of the vehicles. There were armored trucks with .50 caliber weapons, civilian trucks, 18 wheelers with cargo and some carrying gasoline. It was not a difficult decision to pick a vehicle that was not near a gasoline truck. I found some room in the back of a civilian pickup truck where I could toss my duffel bags. I then found a seat in what I figured was the safest truck in the line… an armored truck with a .50 cal on top. I thought I would be in the second truck in the convoy which, in this line of work, is better than being first. Unfortunately, when the convoy started moving, it was my truck that was going to be the first vehicle in the convoy! As I looked around the armored truck to see who may become my battle buddies if things went wrong, I looked up in the turret and saw the .50 caliber was being operated by a female. So much for women not being in combat.

The trip was a 40-minute drive. As I looked at our convoy, I noticed every fifth truck had a .50 caliber machine gun on top. We headed down the three-lane highway that had a wide median and another three lanes running the other way. It was like any other highway, but it had dangerous trash. Trash on the road here was not just tacky but a potential improvised explosive device ("IED"). Even dead animals on the side of the road could have IEDs inside. It was mostly empty fields with shepherds and sheep and a few shacks that dotted the highway. Other than our female gunner waving at some local Iraqis' vehicles on the highway to move away from our convoy, it was an uneventful trip. Luckily, it was not until I arrived at Abu Ghraib that I learned that the convoy was almost canceled today due to an expected attack at Abu Ghraib.

ARRIVING AT ABU

We turned off the highway onto a dirt road leading off on the right. As we came upon a concrete and cyclone fence that created the front entrance of Abu Ghraib, all I could think about was this was like an Iraqi Alamo. Four concrete walls as a perimeter. The front gate was just a rock's throw from the main highway, but the show of force and power was evident. The heavily armed guard towers and concrete barriers that forced vehicles to zig zag around barricades to reach the gate allowed us to get a view of the place that we would call home. As we pulled through the main gate, several large tents could be seen on the right side of the road. Two rows of cyclone fence were all that separated the Iraqi detainees from the rest of the population inside this Iraqi Alamo. As we drove past the detainees, my truck turned left at a "T" in the dirt road and the rest of the convoy turned right. About 20 yards later we came upon what could be described as two warehouse-type buildings on the right side of the road. Their front doors faced each other at a 90-degree angle. Front doors made of plywood protected the hospital inside the warehouse on the left and the warehouse that housed the Abu Ghraib legal office on the right.

    I jumped out of the truck, glad to have made it. Thanked the guys in the truck and the female gunner in the turret. Sometimes it's just the show of force that deters the enemy. Luckily, the guys in the truck knew where the legal office was located, which was good because it was not like there were any signs out front. I entered the warehouse and walked down the hallway made of plywood until I saw a piece of white paper on a plywood door that read, "Task Force 134 Legal Office." I was about to meet other military attorneys and paralegals who had arrived a day or two before. They had been initially spread out across Iraq, but a decision was made to put them all in one place to continue the mission. I was to lead that mission.

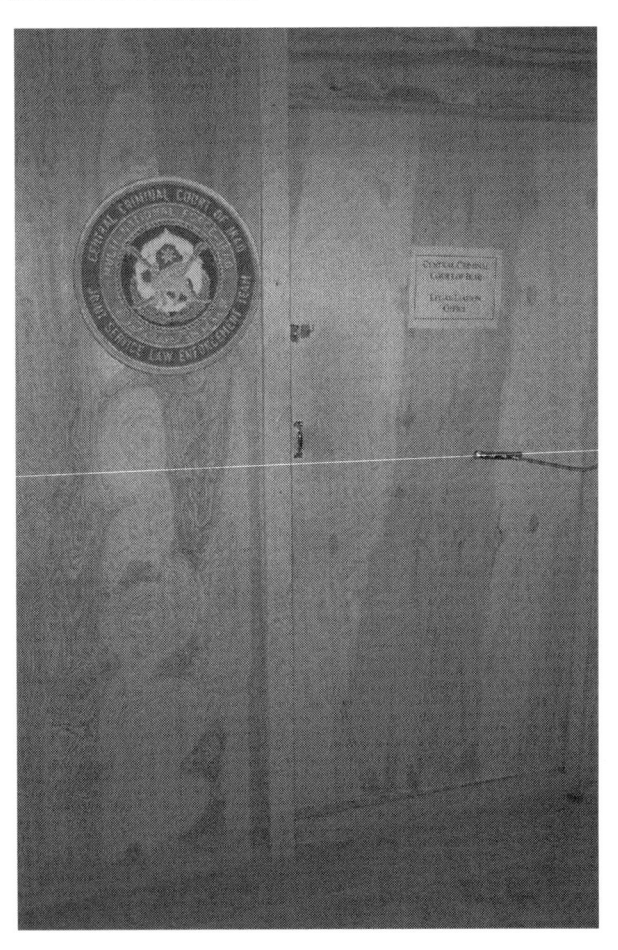

Upon entering through the plywood door, it swung closed behind me by a spring. I observed four long tables with two people sitting at each table. To my left was another door that led to an adjoining office where we would need two desks. The desk on the left would be mine as the officer in charge (OIC). The other desk would belong to my law office manager. On the opposite end of the first room was another door, which led to a room about 20 feet by 20 feet that contained filing cabinets and one large table. Passing through that room led to another room where the attorneys for the Magistrate Cell (Mag Cell) worked. The Mag Cell, as we called it, was an office that determined whether there was probable cause to keep the prisoner detained. If there is probable cause, then the file comes to my office. If there is no probable cause, the detainee is set free. It was manned by one Air Force and one Navy JAG, and two Iraqi translators. The Iraqi translators had been living in the U.S. but decided to return to Iraq as contracted translators to help the U.S. military. If we count the number the rooms from left to right starting with my office as number one, the room with the main entrance as number two, then the storage room is number three and the Mag Cell is number four. The total length had to be less than 80 feet.

There is only one air conditioner for all four rooms. It is located in room number four; therefore, it was important to keep the doors open sometimes. After introducing myself, I ask for a volunteer to help me unload my four duffel bags still on the civilian truck of the convoy. Luckily, before my arrival, my new team had commandeered an old deuce and a half truck, which is what the military calls a 2 ½ ton truck, with no cover on the back. It was old and raggedy and looked like it was from either the 50s or 60s, but it came in handy when it was time to move equipment and supplies like my bags. We loaded my duffel bags and took them to our living quarters, which was across the camp. I will describe our living quarters as a concrete/stucco building that I supposed used to be jail cells when the Iraqis ran this place. My guess comes from the bars on the windows. It could have been a prison hospital I am told.

On the second floor, which is the top floor, we came to a plywood door. We entered a large room about 30 x 15 feet, which contained the only air conditioning unit. Beyond another plywood door was a hallway with five 8 x 6 rooms on each side. My entire team, including two females, lived here. Each person had their own room. My room was the first on the left. It was the biggest because I was the OIC, and it had a window. In most temporary arrangements a window is a good thing. In a war zone, it is not a good thing when your room and window face outwards and stand high above the walls of our Iraqi Alamo and facing towards what appeared to be Iraqi apartment buildings approximately 200 yards away.

I didn't have A/C in my room; none of us did. I did have a fan to circulate the dusty air. I took the liberty of knocking out the broken glass in my window and replacing it with cardboard. I figured the glass would not stop a bullet any more than cardboard, but at least I could remove the cardboard and have a firing position if things got hot. My infantry training came in handy. One of the first things I did was create firing positions for everyone, so when the alarm sounds that the prison is being overrun, we will be able to protect ourselves. I assigned shooters to the front door, side windows, my window, and I put the two females on the back door. That was designed so when we are awakened at night and grab our rifles and put our body armor over our pajamas, the women will not be embarrassingly exposed. I know, it is war, and no one is going to be concerned about what they look like when it is a life or death situation, but I figured removing the distraction would be best for us all.

Now that safety had been established for our living area, it was time to make my 10 x 10 room as comfortable as possible. I shouldn't complain about my room because most of the other guys could stand in the middle of their rooms and touch all four walls. In fact, some could lie in their bed that is against the wall and be able to touch the opposite wall. Anyway, I had a bunk bed and a built-in shelf. I was able to store all my gear on the top bunk and hang my weapons from the bedposts for easy access. I decided I would find the little store on the base to see what I could get to make my living area more comfortable.

At the store, I was able to buy a foam mattress and bedsheets that would fit my bed. I had planned to sleep the next four months in a sleeping bag on top of the mattress, but it gets hot in Iraq even in October and November. I arranged my knick-knacks on the shelf, such as books, keys, and wallet. Because the room was brown on three sides from the unfinished plywood and had a dirty white outside wall, I decided some color would brighten the room up and perhaps make it a "happier" place. I bought some magazines at the store and cut out the pictures and hung them up on my wall. I also bought two small area rugs to keep the dust down and my feet clean. Of course, I hung up the picture my six-year-old son sent with me. It was a cut out of a red apple. Someone had left a picture of Jesus on the wall, so I left that up.

After decorating, it was more colorful but still looked like a jail cell. It had its own plywood door and walls about eight feet tall, but no ceiling except for the roof on the outside building. I looked around at my newly decorated home for the next four months, but before I could pat myself on the back, I hit the concrete floor when I heard the explosion of a mortar.

Outside my cardboard window, I can see a guard tower about 100–150 yards away. The guard towers sat on the inside of the perimeter wall of the prison. Right past the walls are a two-lane road and a very tall building. An ideal place from which to shoot a rocket at our buildings or even the perimeter wall. I was told that the tower shoots someone almost every day when they approach the wall with weapons. I was also told a mortar was fired "the other day" and landed inside the perimeter but didn't hit anything. I half doubted some of these stories, until I saw for myself in just a short amount of time.

Like in most prisons, well I don't know from personal experience, but I presume it occurs, rumors were floating around that there was going to be an escape attempt. This was not the usual kind of prison where prisoners try to break out. Escape from this prison would involve a group of people trying to break into the camp, breaking into the detainee area, and then breaking the detainees out. To give you an idea of the magnitude of the horror that would occur if such a rumor came true, there are over 2,000 Iraqi and foreign fighter detainees here. Needless to say, we have lots of ammo and magazines already loaded for the break-in and breakout.

Anytime we go outside the buildings we were required to wear our body armor (vest and helmet) and carry our weapon. Of course, those at the embassy and Camp Victory can walk around freely without body armor and can go feed fish and swim in Saddam's swimming pool. But not me. My team has to "gear up" to go outside to the water tank to brush our teeth! Have you ever had the experience of walking into a port-a-potty wearing a 30 lb. bulletproof vest, a pistol on your hip, and a helmet on your head? I don't advise it! But it is a good way to lose weight by sweating like you were in a steam room, minus the blue-colored water. I did learn how to spot a good port-a-potty. You see, when I walk inside one and see footprints on the spaces beside the toilet lid, I know this one likely has a "dirty splash." Let me explain. The locals, I learned, will stand up above the toilet and squat down. They don't sit on the toilet. I'm not talking about standing on the floor and squatting over the seat. I mean actually standing on top and squatting. If that was not bad enough, they don't care about "don't squeeze the Charmin" or those cute bears advertising clean rear ends. The locals clean themselves by pouring water in their left hand and splashing it in the "dirty" area. Yep, that is right. Now, you know why the left hand is considered the dirty hand in some countries. I have never seen it or tried it, but I would guess the water splashes everywhere, hence the reason I call it the dirty splash. So, how do you spot a dirty splash? Look for the blue lids of water bottles outside a port-a-potty. That will usually tell you that the person who used it was very thirsty or used the dirty splash method. Another way to tell if the port-a-potty could be dirty is to look for handprints on the outside of the port-a-potty. You see, after putting water on your hand and doing the splash, you have to wipe your wet hand somewhere, right? So, I've witnessed some locals wiping their hand on the wall of the port-a-potty. Just another reason not to touch anything inside or outside a port-a-potty in a third world country.

Living in my 10 x 10 room with no A/C in Abu Ghraib, which is about half-way between Baghdad and Fallujah, where all the heavy fighting was now, wouldn't seem like a discomfort. After all, it was October and should be fall temperatures. I noted on October 12th it was 105 degrees. That encourages you to work late at your office where one A/C is located, even if it has to flow through three offices to reach mine.

After setting up my living quarters, I got a few hours of restless sleep then woke up for a cold shower. The shower area is built to have the sun warm up the water. This is not usually a problem unless you take a shower before the sun comes up! I made my way to the dining facility (DFAC). I must say the best part of any day is mealtime. The DFAC is clean. You have at least five entrée choices and it is all you can eat for free. As sad as it may seem, it is the last meal for some diners. You look around the 50 or so tables filled with military members and civilian contractors enjoying a nice hot meal. Some of the Marines and Army soldiers looked worn and tired but seemed to smile and enjoy themselves being inside a clean room instead of out on the road and in the villages in harm's way.

MEETING MY TEAM

After eating breakfast, I made it to my office and met the two attorneys. One JAG was from the Navy and one JAG was a Marine. We have four paralegals and one security forces member. We have been told by Camp Victory (our HQ) that two other attorneys and one more paralegal would arrive soon. The first order of business was for me to introduce myself as the officer in charge. My message was clear. Make the experience as fun as possible but get the mission accomplished. Everyone was motivated and seemed to be getting along. They all came from around Iraq to assemble in one office. The first ones arrived two weeks ago.

THE JOB

Our mission was to receive files from soldiers who had brought the detainees to Abu Ghraib. The first step in the process is for military intelligence to interrogate the detainee. Then the file goes to the Magistrate Cell, which is the office that connects to mine and is made up of two JAGs and one paralegal. Their job was to review the files that came in and determine whether there's probable cause to detain the prisoner. If there was probable cause, then the file would come to my office, known as the Central Criminal Court of Iraq Legal Liaison or Task Force 134 Legal Office. It was my job, as the OIC, to look at the files to see if there is enough evidence to prosecute the detainee, or whether we needed additional investigation, or whether the case should go to the Combined Review and Release Board who determine whether the detainee should remain in prison due to being a security threat.

The CRRB was my first introduction to the system when I arrived. We quickly learned that the judges at the CCCI want confessions and pictures of the weapons or explosives found with the detainee at the time of capture. If I determined to prosecute the case, then I enter the case into the computer system and provide the file to a JAG in the office to write a prosecution memo setting forth the evidence, to include witness statements. There was one JAG and one paralegal assigned to each geographical area of Iraq. This allowed the JAG/paralegal team to build rapport with the military units in those areas and assist us in collecting the evidence. Luckily, most of them had been out in the field with those units before arriving at Abu Ghraib.

After the prosecution memo is drafted, the case files are transported to the prosecution team at the embassy and the CRRB by way of Camp Victory. Once the files reach Camp Victory, the prosecution files are forwarded to the embassy. It was my office's responsibility to get the files out of Abu Ghraib. The convoy left twice a week from Abu. If a case required more investigation, then the JAG in my office assigned to the area where the detainee was captured contacts the military unit who captured the detainee to collect more evidence. Usually, it involves locating the soldiers who captured the detainee in order to get a witness statement or to interview the soldier to clarify his written statement or to ask if there are any photos we can use as evidence.

Now that the mission was understood, we had to find furniture and equipment for our office. Unlike the embassy and the legal office at Camp Victory, we had to scavenge for items. We were quickly able to obtain two desks and four cushioned chairs from the commander of Abu to add to the two long tables and a bench and four aluminum folding chairs. Now, my office manager and I both had desks. We had to find CDs to back up our files on our computers. We eventually got a second A/C for our office, with one being in my 10 x 10 office. At lunchtime, I started making my way to the dining facility about 60 yards from my office down a dirt/gravel road. On the way, I passed the detainees in yellow jumpsuits who were locked behind two cyclone fences. As soon as I walk out of my building, I'm looking at them across the street. This would be my constant reminder that the cases I work on involve real people.

On my first day at the office, I reviewed about 30 files. We work from 8 am to 6 pm seven days a week. I go back to the office after supper to work until 9 pm to finish up the cases for the day. Afterward,

I head back to the building where I now live. On the first floor, someone set up a room with A/C, darts, a Ping-Pong table, and a room for a big projection TV. Someone rigged it up to receive four channels and it projected onto a whiteboard. It was better than nothing, but after watching 15 minutes of a movie with Russian subtitles starring Matthew McConaughey, I decided to call my family for the first time since leaving home, nine days ago and drop my clothes off at the laundry service here in Abu. The laundry area was just a metal shack that provides netted bags to put your clothes in. You get a receipt, and they take your bag "somewhere" outside of Abu Ghraib to wash your clothes. It took anywhere from two–five days to get the clothes back. It just depended on whether the roads were too dangerous to travel. I was impressed with the way the clothes come back nice and folded, but I'm not sure they used soap because the clothes have no smell. It is a very interesting way to work and live. I find myself constantly looking out for people inside Abu who may pose a threat.

The first Saturday night here I met Major General Geoffrey Miller. After the Abu Ghraib abuse scandal broke in April 2004, he had been appointed as deputy general commander of detainee ops. He had previously been responsible for leading the interrogations at Guantanamo Bay. Later, he would be accused of ordering dogs to be used in enhanced interrogation and other human rights violations. General Miller comes to Abu Ghraib once a week and visits our office while he is here. He works at Camp Victory, but he flies around on a helicopter with no lights. I talked with his assistant, an Army captain. He said that I could fly with one JAG assigned to each section of Iraq to the division headquarters at Tikrit and Mosul. Our office has the country divided up and we need to get face time with the investigators at these divisions who are capturing the bad guys and detaining them before sending them to Abu Ghraib. It would be an opportunity to tell the investigators what kind of information we need from them to get a conviction. I explained that we need to get the word out that the court likes to see pictures of the bad guy posing with his weapons and bombs.

THE ATTACKS BEGIN

October 13, 2004. Wednesday

I was in my room at about 7:30 pm when the electricity goes off. I don't have an A/C in my room, just a fan. So, yes, it is hot. I couldn't read. Probably because I have been reading files all day. I tried to go to sleep, but I can hear machine guns firing that sound like they are right outside my window. I know there are about 100–150 yards from my window to the perimeter, but I can see the perimeter tower from my window. I imagine the tower is most likely doing the shooting. I think back to earlier that day at the office about 3:30 pm when a mortar hit nearby. It shook the whole building. Everyone in the office immediately put on their helmets and body armor. The camp alarm was blaring to warn us of the attack. There are different alarms for different events. When we left the dining hall tonight at about 6 pm, there was shooting towards our office building, then a mortar hit at the far end of the building. It actually landed on a crude volleyball court. I bought a radio today but all I can receive is a bunch of chatting. This is going to be a long four months!

October 14, 2004. Thursday

The day was just a normal working day. The hours do go by fast and we manage to have fun in the office. It seems like every time you turn around it is time to eat. Food! Man, lots of it. Anything and as much as you want. It is a morale booster.

GETTING THE LAYOUT

It is time to explore inside the perimeter of Abu to understand the different groups of people here and their mission. I also want to know the level of threat posed by the locals who live and work within the walls.

My office took a tour around the prison today. Across the dirt road (they are all dirt) from our office there is an Iraqi prison. What I mean is that there is a section where Iraqis are detained for violating every day Iraqi laws, which is separate from the section for those who commit crimes against the coalition forces. Where the local crime violators are kept is referred to as a hard site. It is more like a prison we see back home. It has real walls, ceilings, and bars. They are still inside the perimeter of Abu Ghraib. We got to see the area where the soldiers from a previous military unit abused Iraqi prisoners. The area had a long hallway with jail cells on both sides. The cells are about 10 x 12, which contain a detainee in each. It is said that Saddam would pack up to 100 men into one cell. We walked in the hallway in between the rows of cells full of Iraqi inmates. It is a nasty place. They refer to this area as the "internet cell block" because it was all over the internet when the abuse allegations came out in the news. We also saw the long hallway that has one door at the far end. Back when Saddam was President of Iraq, his guards would tell an inmate that he was being released. This would allow the guard to easily lead the inmate down the hall. The inmate would follow the guard right inside the door at the far end. Unfortunately, instead of the inmate being released from prison, he was released from life. Inside the room, the inmate would be killed with gas. This was said to occur when the cells became too full.

We also toured the area where they cooked for prisoners of the hard site. They heated huge tin tubs over propane tanks. The baking area was surprisingly clean. They had just cooked home-made rolls and one of the locals who was baking picked one up with his bare hands and gave it to us to eat. To keep from offending them and avoid appearing to be the snooty Americans, we ate the roll. I also tried some hot tea that was offered. If I don't get sick, I will be amazed. I guess dying of dysentery is not the most likely way to die in a war zone in this century.

We next toured the area where Uday and Qusay, Saddam's sons, would take inmates and have "fun" with them with their friends. It was a walled off area about 20 x 20 yards that had a little building. The building contained about 10 cells with each about 8 x 4 feet. Each cell had a hole in the floor for a bathroom. The story told is that the two sons would lead a prisoner to a place in the building that contained gallows. We saw the two places on the gallows where the rope would be hung. The inmate would stand on the metal trap doors. The doors would swing down, and the inmate would be hanged. We walked around the area and saw old shoes and other personal items under the trap doors that fell from the prisoners as they met death.

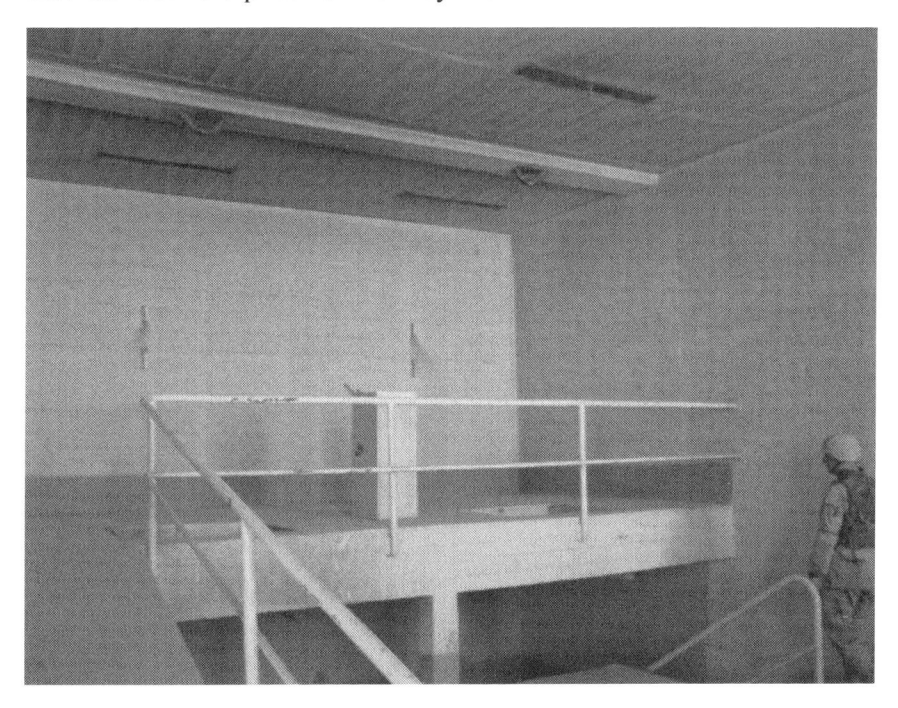

It is said that the two sons would have parties and watch people be hanged. It is weird walking around looking at these places, especially the trap doors and the personal items left behind.

INSIDE THE WALLS OF ABU

Later that day, we drove around the perimeter wall of Abu. I guess Abu Ghraib is about 500 yards in each direction. [I read later it is 280 acres and is 20 miles west of Baghdad] We drove by the towers that the Iraqis are always trying to take out. The towers were shooting flares last night to light up a field outside the wall. We also drove where a mortar hit the other day. It was not far from that same tower. The apartment building across the field from the tower is the one outside my window. They say Marines go inside the apartment buildings every so often and tell the occupants that they will flatten the apartments if any rockets are fired at us from there.

After supper, we went to another section of the second floor of our living area because the Marines that occupied them had left. We went there to scavenge items. I found an old desk there and brought it back to my room. I use the word "desk" very loosely. I also found a homemade footstool that I could put my fan on in my room. I also found an old carpet about 6 x 8; it covers half of my room. I covered the top of my desk and my two shelves with more pages from a magazine. It adds color to the room, but my room is still gloomy even with the Arabic writing on the walls. My staff calls my room a suite because it is twice as big as theirs. I guess it is one advantage of being the boss. The area we live in is called LSA Shadow and the area where we work is called LSA Main. [I still have no idea what LSA stands for. Must be an Army term]. Each section of Abu is surrounded by a wall inside the walls of Abu. So, it's walls inside of the walls. However, the gates to both sections stay open, so they would hardly slow anyone down. Today, we saw a fuel truck parked at the end of our living area. It was a little unsettling. Our living area building is a long wing with rooms on both sides of the hall, kind of like the prison. Luckily, my room was far away from the truck. Today, I decided to look for a dartboard to put in my office to help with morale.

Ramadan starts tomorrow. No one is doing much traveling; although it's a religious holiday, we suspect the bad guys will increase attacks during this time. This should make the next 30 days interesting. Tonight, while in our living areas, we could hear chanting. It was coming from a mosque that I can see from my window. Our interpreter said it was going on too long to be a sermon, so Ramadan may have started early. It was just like what it sounds like on TV.

I found a Mohammad Ali poster and some weights that I can curl. I am slowly making my room more comfortable. I find it kind of fun to go searching for stuff to fix up my room. I have two water bottles as bookends on my shelf. I keep a small bottle by my bed, so I don't have to leave my room in the middle of the night to go to the bathroom. Because to do so would require me to put on my body armor and helmet and walk across a gravel parking area to the port-a-potty. Last night I dreamed I was in a fight and I woke up when I rolled my whole body over and took a wild swing and punched the wall. I had never done that before! I also found a broom and swept my concrete floor in my room. There is sand everywhere. When I come "home" from work, my stereo is covered with very fine dirt. The sand is so fine it is impossible to keep it out of equipment, ears, eyes, or weapons. My windows don't shut or should I say my cardboard does not block out the entire opening, so sand blows in. I note that I will need to work on that before winter comes. I also need a coffee cup with a lid because I am tired of drinking sand. I finish this night sitting in my chair at my new desk drinking a bottle of "near beer." Yes, they give us free non-alcoholic beer to drink.

THE PERKS OF PRISON

October 15, 2004. Friday

I got my laundry back. Not bad since I dropped it off on Wednesday. I take pleasure in the free laundry service and the neatly folded clothes they return to us. Yesterday, I got my hair cut for $3. The best part was they wet your hair when they are finished, and they massage your head. Not just your scalp. They push on your forehead and then slap it and then slap the back of your neck and then rub your head like crazy. Not a gentle thing. Heck, I may go again tomorrow just for the massage! The barbers are Indians who have traveled here to work as civilian contractors. Five of the barbers look like they are from India. I do have to admit the first time the guy started slapping my head I thought he was attacking me. I had thought to myself, *Doesn't this guy know I have a 9mm pistol under this cape?*

We got two new attorneys today at my office, both from the Navy. We also got an Air Force paralegal. We now have a total of nine people and still expecting two more. I am still working on furniture issues, computer hook-ups, and sleeping arrangements for the staff. We have four rooms left in our wing of the building where we live. One of the JAGs that is coming will be assigned to the Magistrate Cell section, so he will live in the other wing of our building where other Magistrate Cell workers live.

We practiced attack responses today and tonight. Tonight, I assigned people to their fighting positions in the living area. Two of the guys and I will guard the front door and fire through the window with bars at anyone who comes up the staircase. I've placed a good shooter at the cardboard window in my room and I placed the security forces member and another shooter in the back room at the end of the hallway and placed two females at the back door. I have a feeling we will be doing this for real before I leave. My infantry training in the National Guard many years ago has come in handy. This same group will be here the entire time of my deployment. Back home, I am a deputy staff judge advocate where I am responsible for supervising a legal office with six attorneys and six paralegals. Although the legal office I supervise at Abu is about the same size, it is very different in a combat/war environment. Everyone in my office is taking the attack and fire positions seriously. It is kind of funny because, except for the one Air Force military cop, we are all attorneys and paralegals and may be taking this task more seriously than full-time soldiers. We turn our lights out and man our positions. This was a designated time for the entire base to prepare their fighting positions. We have turned off our lights and manned our positions, but we still see people walking to the showers. I believe some people are too complacent, but not my office. The next senior JAG in my office, my number two if you will, is a Navy JAG. I use him as a deputy staff judge advocate. He is real gung-ho, which I didn't expect from a Navy JAG in the middle of the desert! I'm still a little confused about the Navy being here!

The mosque outside the Abu walls was lit up tonight. I can see it from my room. A lot of loud praying from there tonight. It is the first day of Ramadan, and I hope the loud praying doesn't last as long as last night. I bought a dartboard for the office today. Tomorrow will be long because we have to wait for the two-star general to come visit. One of the paralegals just bought a 15-inch screen laptop. We will watch movies tomorrow night at the office. As I finish my near-beer at 9:30 pm, I talk to the new JAG and listen to one of the few CDs I have. The radio only picks up Iraqi stations, so the CD helps block out the noise from the mosque, which kind of scares me. It makes me think of the Native Americans singing before they attacked the cowboys in the old movies.

WAKE UP CALL

October 16, 2004. Saturday

Well, guess what? I was suddenly awakened at 5:25 am to the sound of small arms fire, which means M-16s were being fired as opposed to a heavy gun, such as M240 or .50 calibers. It was loud, it was fast, and it was close. We jumped up and started telling everyone in our living area to get up and, "Man the battle stations." Now that I look back on it, it kind of sounds like something you would hear in *Star Wars*! We grabbed our body armor, helmets, and weapons and ran to our fighting positions just like we had practiced. We learned that there was a sniper firing from the apartments right outside the perimeter wall. The apartments that overlook the walls! The ones I can see from my room! The two guard towers that face those apartments lit them up. Then, two more towers clear across the base starting firing over our building towards the apartment. While the firefight was going on between the towers and the sniper in the apartment building, a convoy passes Abu on its way down the highway. The convoy thought they were being attacked and may have fired on the guard towers. This is what they call the fog of war. We also heard someone firing immediately outside our window. It's not all sorted out, yet.

Tonight, the two-star general came to our office at 8 pm. We were watching the movie *Black Hawk Down* on the paralegal's new laptop.

We had watched most of it when we were told the General's helicopter was on its way, so the officers and I had to go meet the two-star general at the helipad. After the meet and greet with the two-star, the officers and I went back to the office. The General sleeps in our building and usually stops by our office before bedtime. The law office manager and I stayed at the office until 10:40 pm but sent everyone else home at 10 pm. The General didn't come by the office as we were told, so we left and went back to our rooms. I directed everyone to get to the office early in the morning just in case the General came by. It is 11 pm and I'm tired. I did develop a schedule, so each team has a day off a week. I think this will keep up morale, which is a necessity for maximum performance.

October 17, 2004. Sunday

Just a quick note because I am extraordinarily tired. I got off work today at about 11:30 am. I went back to my room after lunch and took a nap. I woke about 5 pm and dropped my laundry off and then headed to the office to call home. I was about 40 feet outside the door of the building where my office is located when mortars hit! Boom! Boom! Boom! Boom! Boom! Eight to 10 times. The base alarm system went off. I pushed my way into the door to get inside so I could take up a fighting position. I waited a few minutes until everything was quiet. I got up and went into my office and called home. During the call, the base alarm went off again. More mortars hit! I continued my call home because that was important. I am hoping my family can't hear the explosions in the background. All is well at home. The kids got a dog! That did not take long! My six-year-old son got a bike for his birthday while I was gone, although his birthday is not until the 26th. My 13-year-old daughter had gone to Six Flags with friends. Tonight, I also sent my first email to my parents and my office back home letting everyone know I was safe and assure them I am not in any danger. Although you want to share these adventures with your family, you must wait until you are safely home, so they are not worried. I didn't know at this time that two weeks after my return there would be a death in my immediate family.

October 18, 2004. Monday

Nothing extraordinary happened today. I did go talk to Colonel Thomas, the commander of Abu Ghraib, about something the field artillery group that occupies the first floor of the building in which we live said yesterday. I heard them say they have people coming back from the field and would be taking over our living area upstairs. In essence, my team would have to change living areas. Colonel Thomas assured me that he had promised our office a place to live and we have it. He said no one is making my office move unless the General orders it. The two-star general comes to our building each week and sometimes meets with us, so we have a good chance of convincing him not to order us to move. Also, my boss, Colonel Phelps, is the General's legal advisor. While talking to Colonel Thomas, I was able to convince him to buy a carpet for our office to keep the sand and dust from flying around and getting into our laptops. He told me to provide his Sergeant with the measurements and he would take care of it.

On the way back from supper tonight, there was a mortar attack again. Luckily, this time there was only one, but it landed on a basketball court only 50 yards from our living area. Of course, no one plays basketball because it would be difficult to dribble up and down the court and shoot while wearing 30 lbs. of body armor and a weapon strapped to your leg. Now that I think about it, it would be a funny sight to see! Unfortunately, the mortar injured three people. One of the females in our office was in the shower near the target and ran out. She saw an injured soldier yell, "I've been hit." She was able to call for a medic. I heard another guy was seriously injured. I don't know about the third injured person.

Tonight, we heard another mortar. It hit across the gravel parking lot from our living area. The best way I can describe what it sounds like and feels like when a mortar hits, is to imagine standing by your front door and someone slams a sledgehammer into the other side of the door. The sound startles you, but the energy causes not only the room to shake but your whole body to shake. It is powerful. The further away the mortars land, of course, decreases the amount that the room, ground, and your body shakes. I will also try to describe the area where we are living and working.

My living area is on the second floor. The building is inside a walled-off area but doesn't have a gate. Across the street from my office are 1500 prisoners and Iraqi staff in the hard site prison. On the other side of the hard site are 2000 detainees being held in tents surrounded by a metal chain-link fence for committing crimes against the coalition. The whole prison (Abu) is only about 500 yards squared. There is probably 200 yards between my living area and my office that we walk every day. There are probably about 60 yards from my office to the dining facility. I heard today that the building where we live used to be a prison hospital, at least the first floor was. The guys downstairs moved in eight months ago and found skeletons and bones. This makes sense. We have metal hooks in our ceilings. I don't mean the small kind your grandma uses to hang plants from the ceiling of the porch. I am talking about the big hooks that could hold a side of beef or a human body. I actually have one of these steel hooks hanging from the ceiling in my room. I'm sure I will sleep better tonight thinking about a dead body that used to hang from the hook here. On the side of the dining hall, there used to be a wall that has now been torn down. The story is that prisoners were lined up against that wall and executed. I have learned way too much about this place today.

October 19, 2004. Tuesday

We found out today what happened in our living area last night. We were told that an Army captain got hit in the stomach, intestines, and diaphragm from the shrapnel of the mortar. He took a turn for the worse last night and had to be intubated. There were four ordinances (UXOs) that didn't explode. It seems like the enemy has our living area in their sights. They hit us every night between 4 pm and 7 pm, then they celebrate. We were getting ready to leave the office at 5:45 pm today and we heard an RPG or something. It flew low and whistled and then thud! No explosion. I hadn't heard a whistle like that before. It shook our office door. I waited about 20 minutes then walked to the dining facility. No one else in my office wanted to leave the building after hearing the mysterious flying object. They all decided to skip supper. They just sat there in the office with their helmets and body armor on. You just have to be careful. The rule at Abu is if you are outside a building, regardless of if it is inside the walls, you still must wear your body armor. That means even going outside to stand against the wall for sunlight you have to be suited up. All lieutenant colonels and above must have their weapons locked and loaded at all times. Usually, we don't put a magazine into the weapons until we hear the alarm go off. Not anymore.

I started making an air duct to get the air conditioner to blow from the front room of our living area to my room. I've been cutting and taping water bottles together to connect to the air conditioner. I think I may need about 12 more bottles. Heck, it may be time for heat in our building by the time I finish. I have been at Abu for one week. The work is steady, but not too hard.

One of the enlisted guys brought me his Metallica CD because he is tired of hearing my country music. I have been playing my Josh Turner CD, *Long Black Train*, every morning and night. I figured Josh Turner would be a good CD to listen to in war because he was a former

Marine. Well, my staff is happy that I am jamming to heavy metal now. They keep asking each other, "Is he listening to heavy metal?" "Who is jamming to Metallica?" I guess going from Josh Turner's "Long Black Train" to Metallica's "Enter Sandman" is a big change. But this deployment is all about adapting to the circumstances and being successful outside your comfort zone.

THE GHETTO HAS A VISITOR

October 20-21, 2004. Wed-Thurs

The General came in a helicopter to see the guys wounded from the latest attack. My boss, Colonel Phelps came, too. He wanted to see our sleeping area and was shocked to see that it looked so "ghetto." He told us to give him a list of whatever we wanted to fix up our area, rugs, carpet, TV, etc. I don't think he realized how run-down it was. He had us load some of our files from our office for him to take back on the chopper. Lt. Faulkner, the Navy JAG, and I carried them to the helipad. On our way out, we passed the General and his entourage. The General stopped us, laughed, and said, "Look, lawyers carrying boxes… anyone have a camera?" He seems to like us. The base commander, Colonel Thomas, said later that we were some high-price box holders. Colonel Phelps talked to us and said it was my office and he wasn't going to tell me how to get the job done. He wanted us to go out and talk to troops in the field about how to conduct investigations. He told us to set it up ourselves. Find a convoy that is going out and find one coming back. It is almost like hitchhiking. I've been taking pictures on the digital camera and sending them home.

The people sleeping on the floor below us have more people coming in. So do the people in the wing next to us. They told us that we would have to move. I went and talked to Colonel Thomas about it. He said we won't have to move. A sergeant from downstairs just came out and asked me if I had thought about what we are going to do when his troops get here. I said we are not moving. He was mad and asked who said, and I told him, Colonel Thomas. He said they were going to fight the decision, so we will just have to see.

Back in my room, I am drinking another can of "near beer." I have to get up at 4:30 am to go and call the kids between 5–6 am my time, which will be 8–9 pm their time. I am catching a Black Hawk helicopter on Sunday to go to Baghdad, specifically Camp Victory for a meeting with the head attorney at the embassy legal office to talk about what we need as evidence to win a conviction in court. We received three seats on the chopper. The odd thing is we started watching the movie *Black Hawk Down* last Saturday night and going to finish it this Saturday night while waiting on the General to make his weekly visit. Military members are known to have a dark sense of humor, perhaps to prevent emotions from interfering with the objectivity needed to perform the job. The General sleeps right down the hall from our office, so he usually drops by on the way to bed. You can tell where he sleeps because there is an armed guard outside his door.

October 22, 2004. Friday

Well, today was my day off. However, I got up at 4:30 am to go to the office to call my wife and kids. It was eerie walking across the dirt field with the orange lights reflecting off the dust in the sky and hearing ole "Mohammad" on the loudspeaker at the mosque across the street chanting. No one else is walking around at this time. I ended up working most of the day at the office.

SPACE INVADERS

A senior master sergeant in the Army came by the office today. He told me his guys were coming back and wanted their living spaces back. Of course, we are living there now. I told him we were not moving. I can't voluntarily move my people. If the base commander wants us to move then fine, but we had already talked to Colonel Thomas. The Senior Master Sergeant didn't understand that we only have one wing and the other wing was open. Our Marine JAG went with the Senior Master Sergeant to show him our space and the vacant space where he could put his people. The Senior Master Sergeant said fine, he wouldn't press the issue. I know that the MSgt who came by the day before had told the Senior Master Sergeant, who is a higher rank, to come by to pressure us.

Two staff sergeants from the legal office at Camp Victory are coming tomorrow with money. They are going to buy us stuff for our living area, such as a TV, DVD player, heater, rugs, chairs, etc. I priced stuff today at the little store. I would love to have a coffee cup with a lid to keep the sand out of my coffee, but the store doesn't have any. Tomorrow is supposed to be violent. It has something to do with the moon phases, I'm told, but I don't really understand it. Perhaps those without night vision goggles can maneuver better in the moonlight. I don't believe science has shown that a full moon makes people more violent. The Iraqis are supposed to attack us tomorrow and on the 28th. Also, the perimeter guard towers are looking for volunteers to man the towers so the Marines can go to a Marine celebration on the 10th of November. It's the Marines' birthday. I am going to volunteer. Well, I'm going to drink one more near beer. I figured action will start after midnight. Oh yea, I worked on my air conditioning duct. I'm taping water bottles together to get cold air from the air conditioner in the day room to my room about 40 feet away. I need about 49 bottles, which is more than I had originally thought. I now have 32. Working on this project does help pass the time. There is something therapeutic about cutting off both ends of plastic water bottles and taping the bottles together. It has been about 105 degrees every day since I got here, but I'm worried about getting cold in the winter.

October 23, 2004. Saturday

The General decided to not come in until tomorrow, so I let everyone leave the office early. Sometimes travel is changed due to threat assessments. I stayed at the office visiting with a lieutenant colonel from the Army Judge Advocate General's Office (the office of the top JAG of the Army) who had come by at the end of the day. We were all cleaning our weapons because I made a rule to do it every Saturday night. The Lt. Colonel came by about 5:30 pm, and seemed like a nice guy but wanted a rundown on how we operate and the function, mission, etc. Everyone else was gone, so about 6:40 pm I told him I had to go eat because the chow hall closes at 7 pm. He was fine with it, so I jumped in our Humvee and drove to get my laundry before it closed at 7 pm. I guess clean clothes were more of a priority than eating, especially when you sweat through your clothes every day and then re-wear the same outfit for a few days. I was able to make it to the chow hall in time to eat.

We got the Humvee today. We will have to give up our deuce and a half. The Humvee has four doors and is armored. It is a military police vehicle.

PROBLEMS IN THE OFFICE

I had a staff meeting today. We had some issues with one of the enlisted guys acting like he knew about computers, but it seems to me he wants to be in control. He is the only one whose laptop has the NIPR net (non-secure internet protocol router), which is for unclassified information, and the only one we can use to send emails to our families. The rest of the laptops are called SIPR (secure internet protocol router) and are for classified information only, such as information regarding the current threat assessment, our case files and travel coordination with Camp Victory. He is also the only paralegal with a computer, but he is the most junior in the office, an E4. The other paralegals share a computer with the JAG on their team. Now that we have the Humvee, the young paralegal also thinks he is the only one qualified to drive it. His tone is almost condescending. He is a nice guy, but his know-it-all attitude is causing problems. When you work together and live together for four months, you can't afford to have any issues that cause dissension.

During our office staff meeting, I re-emphasized that this is my office. I welcome opinions and suggestions but if they can't voice their opinion with respect and follow customs and courtesies of the military, then I will shut them down and shut them out. I told them I run a relaxed atmosphere office and I encourage humor and excitement, but they must balance that with the realization and seriousness that we are in a combat zone and people are trying to kill us. I told them my leadership style is the way I told them the first day I arrived. I give them enough rope, i.e. discretion to get the job done. With that rope, they can either hang themselves or make a beautiful lasso. My leadership style is to tell you what I want to be accomplished and let you figure out how. To me, that is leadership as opposed to management. I told them if they can't use good discretion, then I can run a tight ship and start a dictatorship-style office and that wouldn't be much fun.

TIGHTENING UP

I, here is the funny part, told them I own the Humvee. I don't mind if people want to use it as long as they are trained to drive it. I will make sure everyone receives training. However, before it can leave the office and go to the dining facility or our living area, I must be in it. Before it can leave our living area, dining facility, or office, I must be in it. I don't care who drives or I can drive because I already have a Humvee license (I made sure I was qualified before I left home) and drove one for many years when I was in the infantry. So, I think I need to tighten up the reigns a little bit on the guys. However, the non-commissioned officer in charge (NCOIC), who is the senior leader of the enlisted paralegals, asked me to give him a few days to see if he can get it all straightened up. My NCOIC, i.e. law office manager, is Air Force MSgt Chris Brown. He is a standup guy. As the NCOIC he is the go-between between the officer-in-charge (me) and the enlisted members of the staff. The paralegals are enlisted members, and the attorneys are the officers. It is my role to deal directly with the officers.

Tomorrow, I fly on a Black Hawk and catch one back on Tuesday. Oh, with the Humvee, we can join the Army convoy anytime to go anywhere. It is dirty but has a new engine. Oh, only a couple of mortars hit today, not the heavy attack we were bracing for. This is the first time in a couple of days.

October 27, 2004. Wednesday

Last Sunday, I flew in a Black Hawk helicopter to the "green zone." That is the area around the palaces in Baghdad that is relatively safe due to coalition forces operating checkpoints. It took almost 20 mins to complete the flight from Abu to Baghdad. The chopper flew low and fast. It zigzagged a lot because it was daytime and that is the evasive maneuver it uses to avoid any potential missile attacks and small arms fire. When we landed, the paralegals from the embassy picked us up from the airfield and took us to catch the Rhino that would take us to Camp Victory. We had to go on Route Irish to get to Camp Victory. We had a couple of armored trucks with gunners in our convoy. When traffic got bad, we cut across the medians in the road and went against oncoming traffic and then cut over again. These roads are like three and four lanes wide. We could hear the radio near our driver and the truck upfront calling out what he saw on the route. For example, "Hodgee" on left, parked car on right, two "Hodgees" in median, overpass clear. Hodgee is slang for a civilian Iraqi, which was later learned is often used in an insulting manner.

Camp Victory was more relaxed than Abu and nice to visit. No body armor requirement, although a guy from the State Department was killed there the day before. A mortar had hit the shower shack where he was taking a shower. One of our paralegals was 50 yards away and ran with a fire extinguisher. He checked on the guy along with a medic. The guy had caught shrapnel in the back of his head and died.

OBLIGATORY THRONE SHOT

We visited the palace at Camp Victory and took pictures of us sitting on Saddam's throne, like many other soldiers who visited the palace had done. There must be hundreds, if not thousands of pictures of American soldiers sitting on Saddam's throne. I also took pictures of the palace balcony and the golden toilet. We went to the First CAV office and gave a briefing to their attorneys about how to check the file for proper evidence before sending the detainee's file to my office. We told them what the Iraqi court likes and requires to convict a detainee. There were some guys in the Arkansas National Guard there. One was two years ahead of me in law school. His name was Captain Zega. We ate real good there; crab legs and steak. I talked to a Lt. Colonel who was a JAG in the Army. He told us that he goes out with special forces dressed like a local in a dishdasha (but we often referred to it as a man-dress) and fake mustache but wears his uniform underneath. They do close recon and then execute the kill. While sitting in the car advising the special forces, he only needs to look like a local from the waist up.

I got my head shaved while I was there. I shaved all of it and took pictures. I bought my daughter and wife jewelry boxes at a bizarre from some local vendors. I bought my son some Iraqi money that was used when Saddam was president.

We flew back to Abu late last night; actually, this morning at 2:15 am on a Chinook helicopter. A Chinook is a large helicopter with two propellers. It only took six minutes to fly from BIAP to Abu. Marines fly at night without lights, perhaps because they are large and slow. The back end of the Chinook stayed open, so we could see the helicopter behind us zigzagging like us. It was pretty cool. For some reason, looking out the back of the helicopter at the houses below reminded me of old Vietnam War era songs, like "Fortunate Son" by Creedence Clearwater Revival.

While at Camp Victory, we went to Saddam's boathouse, which was only a few hundred yards from the legal office on the lake. He had three crappy boats, but I still took pictures of them. One though was a nice wooden ski boat like they had back in the 1930s. We also went swimming in his pool that was a few blocks away from his palace on the lake. We played water volleyball and basketball in the pool and threw the football. It had like a tent on top of the pool. The water was so freaking cold even though it was 100 degrees outside. We met two guys at the pool who were ITT employees doing contract work with telephones. They let us use their computer and DVDs at night to watch movies. One had a huge screen on his computer. We watched *We Were Soldiers* which is a movie about the Vietnam War, and *13th Warrior* starring Antonio Banderas. I'm not sure why the movies we watch in the combat zone are about war! We drank near beer and fell asleep.

Colonel Phelps seems pleased with the work of our office. He liked the evidence collection card my office created. These are little cards that contain information on how the soldiers should collect evidence on a detainee, such as take pictures of the weapons and take pictures of the detainee with the weapons, write specific details in the witness statements, etc. We plan to pass these out to soldiers who bring us detainees. He made a couple of suggestions and said to make the changes and email them to him. He wanted to print more and laminate 100,000 of them to put in the field all across Iraq. I felt really good about that. Well, I'm going to read and then crash for the night. Bugs are eating me up at night. I've got dozens of sores on me like scratched mosquito bites. I took my sheets to the laundry today, so I'll sleep on my sleeping bag, since I don't have spare sheets.

Yesterday was my son's seventh birthday! Second family member's birthday I missed so far.

READING THE TEA LEAVES

October 29, 2004. Friday

    I learned some interesting facts today or yesterday; days tend to run together over here. Forty percent of the Iraqi correctional officers haven't been showing up for work. I wonder if they know something we don't know…like a potential attack coming? Recently, we had someone who came to visit one of the detainees and swap places; the detainee walked out of the prison. However, the real detainee is coming to visit, so we will be able to catch him. Also, the third-ranking guy for Abu Musab Al-Zarqawi, a known terrorist, came to visit a detainee and now he is a detainee! Not real smart, huh? There is a brick wall that is halfway built between the hard site prison and my office. No one has been working on it, though. We found out that the Iraqi foreman was killed, and the workers are scared to work on it. So, only a cyclone fence surrounds the hard site prison building from the rest of the base. Also, I learned that the Iraqi correctional officers, prison guards, are the only ones on duty between 5 pm and 8 am every night. So, if there is going to be a breakout, it will most likely be during that time. During the day, we have coalition forces at the hard site helping and teaching the Iraqi correctional officers how to do their job.

    October 28, 2004, was supposed to be a bad day, but not much happened on the base. There were four improvised explosive devices (IED) attacks at four different places last night… all within two miles of Abu. We heard the explosions and found out today what they were. We were also told that rocket attacks would occur today or tonight. Last night and tonight were full moons and very illuminating. We saw our guys illuminating an area outside Abu while we were walking to supper. Hopefully, this will keep the bad guys from getting close enough to shoot at us with an RPG.

I sent our Marine JAG and two paralegals in our Humvee to join a convoy that was headed to Camp Victory, so they could get supplies and have a little rest and relaxation. They will be back tomorrow afternoon. Today was my day off. I just slept one hour later and got to work five minutes later than the days I do work. After lunch, I went back to my room to take a nap. About two hours later, the Navy paralegal from my office woke me up because Colonel Phelps called and wanted to talk to me. I got dressed and went to the office to call him and guess what? He can't remember what he wanted to tell me! We all thought it was funny, so I just stayed at the office and worked.

REAL BLOOD FOR HALLOWEEN

October 31, 2004. Sunday

Well, I'm extremely tired today and not feeling well. I stayed at the office until 10:30 pm last night with the other attorneys waiting for the General, who didn't show up again. I let the paralegals go home at 8:30 pm. At the office, we watched a movie about Halloween. Instead of trick or treating with my kids, I sit in the desert doing what they call "service before self."

Today, was just a meeting day. I guess it is one way to break up the routine. At a briefing today it was announced that we are supposed to get hit tonight at midnight. Yesterday, eight Marines were killed outside the walls of Abu in a convoy when a suicide vehicle exploded. The word was the Marines would be brought to Abu, but they didn't come. Today, some Marines were shot, and they came to the hospital, which is right beside our office. When I was going outside today, I saw some Marines pulling up in a Humvee and one was vomiting or very upset. Then, an ambulance unloaded a Marine on a stretcher…he didn't look good. There are more Marines on base these last few days. They must be getting ready to go attack some place.

My office took our group pictures today that came out pretty good. It is strange how some people are injured while some only have close calls and some are safe. It reminds me of a saying we had as a kid:

"Close only counts in horseshoes and grenades." I guess I mean that the bad guy doesn't have to aim at you or hit you to harm you. They only have to land the mortar close to you because the shrapnel and combustion will do the job. Although we try to enjoy ourselves while performing our duties, we don't make light of the fact that others have it much worse than we do. My friends from the National Guard unit back home are currently in Baghdad, Iraq. They are infantry, so their mission is a lot more dangerous. It isn't lost on me how fortunate I am to be working at the prison as an attorney while my high school friends are now in harm's way.

Here at Abu, we complain and become afraid when the mortars land nearby and shake the walls, but we are thankful we aren't having to endure what these soldiers are facing in the villages and the outposts. We see the exhausted looks on their faces that hide their pain while they smile and laugh with each other in the dining facility. There is a visible change that occurs to people who have been in a combat zone. A person can look at before and after photos of soldiers on the internet and see the hollow look in their eyes caused by the horrors they have experienced.

The Marine JAG decided to pay for half a TV and the rest of us pitched in $10. We borrowed the Navy paralegal's DVD player, so now we can watch movies in the "day room" of our living area. Some guys from the civil engineering office came to our living area and put wood on two of our windows that were busted out. I had garbage bags and cardboard on the open window to keep out the wind and sand. Everything in my room is covered in dust.

I got my care package last night. My son drew pictures, and both my kids made frames for pictures. They looked great! My wife had put together a photo album and some framed pictures. They sent me candles and deodorizers. It smells nice in my room now. I also received

CDs and a stuffed cat that looks like our pet cat Ozzy. I'm about 25% finished with this deployment. I try not to think too much about home or I will miss everyone and everything too much. It was great talking to my kids and wife tonight. I got to wish my daughter a happy birthday. Her birthday is actually on Halloween. I can't believe she is 14 years old! Well, I'm tired and need to crash. It is 9:21 pm. Third family member's birthday I have missed on this deployment.

ESCAPE ATTEMPT

November 3, 2004. Wednesday

    It has been a couple of days since I have written in my journal. A lot has happened. Yesterday there was a pretty big attack. Mortars were going off shaking our office building then small arms fire right outside our office door. Keep in mind that my office is only about 60 feet from the hard site prison. Only a barbed wire fence or one door (depending on where they come from) separates them from the rest of us. When we heard the shots, we loaded up (put on our vests and helmets). I stepped into the hallway to ask other occupants of the building, which happened to be security forces, what was going on. They told me we were in REDCON 1, the highest alert. We also went to Condition Amber, which means everyone inserts a loaded magazine into your weapons. My office is responsible for guarding the rear door of the building that houses our office (opposite end of building away from the hard site prison). I guess they were smart assigning the lawyers to the back door. I went to the rear door and took two guys with me. The rear door was opened, so we looked out. We could hear shots being fired about 50 feet away from us. It seemed to be coming from the guard tower. I had a radio on my vest and was scanning frequencies to monitor the action. I heard detainees had escaped and were running west, which is toward our building. I also heard the radio say they were either naked or in orange or yellow jumpsuits. Yellows are the anti-coalition detainees who are kept in the tents. Orange is what the Iraqi criminals in the hard site wear. After about 30 minutes of gunfire, it was over.

Also, during the action, the radio said one KBR employee was shot in the abdomen. KBR is a contracting company that provides base services such as dining hall facilities. Their employees are civilians from the U.S., Iraq, or other foreign country who are willing to work in a combat zone. After the attack was over, we learned that on Route Mobile (the street running outside Abu) two U.S. convoys passed each other at the exact time an IED exploded. Then firing from about twenty Iraqis began. The perimeter towers fired back as well as some inner towers. At the same time, the detainees in the hard site tried to riot, so one of the towers fired shots at them. Unconfirmed reports said some Iraqis were hit. The KBR employee was coming out of the shower and took a bullet in the stomach. He was an American. He died a few minutes later. His vest wouldn't have saved him because the shot was low. It isn't clear if the shot was fired from outside the base or not. They said all detainees were accounted for and none escaped. I heard there were supposedly a couple of days this week that Iraqis believed they can't be killed, and if they are killed as a martyr, they get 72 virgins in heaven. I have no idea if these things are true or just part of the everyday chatter you hear in close quarters with a bunch of soldiers. I'm more than happy to help him die for his country so I don't have to die for mine. We heard word before that they were going to try to IED one place on the perimeter wall, and then while we were distracted try to breach the perimeter in another area. Mortars are expected, but when you hear small arms fire, then that usually means they are inside our perimeter or very close.

In the dining facility hung a picture of the KBR employee who was killed. They are having a memorial. KBR runs the dining and laundry services.

November 4, 2004. Thursday

Well, just a normal day. Rain stopped. When it rains, it rains hard. All the roads on Abu are dirt, so you can imagine the mess it makes. We walk a lot within the perimeter, so avoiding mud puddles is impossible. The whole place is like one huge mud puddle. When it isn't raining, sometimes the sky will turn orange because a sandstorm is coming. If you are outside, you want to put your goggles on if you cannot reach a building. If you are caught outside, you will not only be covered in very fine sand, but will be picking it out of your eyes, nose, ears, and hair for a long time. Got my door fixed today. I had to get one inch of the bottom cut off so it would close. It was warped after taking a beating with a sledgehammer or extreme kicking. When and under what circumstances are unknown. Tomorrow is supposed to be a bad day. Two people at different times reported that a three-prong attack is planned for Abu tomorrow. Using indirect fire, vehicle borne improvised explosive device (VBIED) and small arms fire. They are supposed to use the bombs that blow up before they hit the ground so it has a bigger kill area. One of the Iraqi correctional officers (ICO) belongs to the group suspected in the coming attack. The same ICO was busted for taking pictures inside Abu in September. Colonel Phelps is supposed to come tomorrow, so I told him about the report so he will be aware of it. Not sure why he is coming. The small arms fire we heard yesterday was insurgents firing at the port-a-potty trucks right outside our wall. That is kind of low to try and deny us of clean toilets! We need to add that to the rules of war. I was walking along a dirt road and passed some of the detainees in a tent section (where they go before being released). Then I heard the shots. Nothing on the other side of the tent area but the outside wall. I can see through the tent area and see the wall.

SHARING THE TOILET

The third-country nationals and locals have been using all eight port-a-potties that are right outside my office. Two are for patients. You can tell when they use it because there are muddy footprints up by the lid because they squat and don't sit. They get crap all over the place. So, we put up signs on all of the port-a-potties, except one. The sign said U.S. Military/DoD personnel only. Then one said TCN/HCN (host country national) authorized only. Unfortunately, it wasn't a popular decision, so we had to remove the signs and take our chances. My head is very stuffy now. I need to take more Sudafed. I have a feeling my throat will be sore tomorrow. I woke up last night at midnight because ole Mohammad was getting at it on the loudspeaker at the mosque right outside Abu. None of us knew who it was, what he was saying, or why. Man, he is driving me nuts! He does it for like three hours!

November 6, 2004. Saturday

Well, nothing happened yesterday like we had heard. We had plans. This is one time in which broken plans are a good thing. I took three of the guys to the front door of our work area to set up a better fighting position. Although the best fighting position is outside, there are two problems. One is mortars and the second is the Marines in the towers. We have been told that Marines will shoot just about anything moving. So, we created a firing position in the second doorway inside and moved a freezer out a little bit to get a fighting position behind it. The ceiling will probably withstand 80mm mortar, but there is only plywood going across the top of the wall where there used to be windows to the building.

I did learn yesterday, after talking to a Navy investigator who investigates detainees' allegations of abuse, that the KBR worker who got shot in the stomach a couple of days ago was over by the NW corner of the base (I can see it from my room). The KBR worker had heard small arms fire and opened the door to his room to see what was going on, and when he did, he took one to the stomach. So, the story about him coming out of the shower wasn't accurate. The angle of the shot was such that they could tell it came from the outside of the wall. They just shot over the wall and the bullets dropped in on us. His body armor probably wouldn't have saved him. Well, today is a long day/night because the General is coming and we stay at the office until he gets here. Today is the one-month anniversary that I left home. I think time will start going fast; I hope.

PREPARING FOR THE TOWER

November 9, 2004. Tuesday

    Still fighting this cold and headache. Trained on the M240B, which is like a squad assault weapon, but more sophisticated and shoots a 7.62mm round. I volunteered to work the perimeter guard tower tomorrow from 2 pm to 4 pm, so the Marines who work the towers can celebrate the birthday of the USMC. I picked Tower 1. It is on the NW corner. It is the one that looks like a deer stand. It has two rows of sandbags for protection. It has two M240s and binoculars and we will have our M-16s or GAUs, too. Tower 9 will be on my left and closer to the houses outside the base. Tower 1 gets shot at from the palm trees on the right. The battle of Fallujah has kicked off. Last night we heard the bombs dropping. Fallujah is about 12 miles to the west. It sounds like thunder clapping. We heard it all day today, too. It is about 8:30 pm.

    We just got attacked! We heard a mortar go off and then a second one real close that shook our building. The sirens on base went off, so we turned off the lights and grabbed our body armor and weapons and manned our positions in our living area. If there are multiple mortars, then we go downstairs to the bottom floor of our living quarters to a little room for better protection. The first report was the mortar hit inside the base. But I believe it was determined that it didn't. I'll know more tomorrow. One of the Marines across the hall was running down the stairs and fell. I think he may have broken his arm. Again, I'll know more tomorrow. My head is killing me. I keep taking Sudafed during the day and Nyquil at night. I just took another Motrin. I have been feeling run down the last few days. The night before last I went to sleep at 7 pm. We got attacked and the guys had to wake me up. I slept through the mortar attack! Thank you, Nyquil! Not sure that would make a good commercial, "Helps you get a good night's rest even while the enemy is attacking!"

I've got to get my energy back, so I can get in a routine for the gym. I have only been once since I arrived. I need to try to go in the mornings, but I have to hurry so I don't miss all the water in the shower. Well, tomorrow will be exciting. I feel good about volunteering to help out in the tower. The towers are the first line of defense for the base. Lt. Faulkner, the Navy JAG, will be in Tower 1 with me. The Marines said that the sandbags come up to your throat inside the tower and then there is a roof to the tower. So, unless a sniper gets me or a mortar or RPG, I should be safe in a small-arms firefight.

The Marines are celebrating the birthday of the Marines and asked for volunteers to work the towers for a couple of hours. The funny thing is our Marine JAG adamantly opposed to working in the tower. So, only the Navy JAG and I will volunteer from my office. The whole office thinks we are crazy for volunteering. I feel that I trained for eight years in the infantry for this type of thing, so it makes logical sense that I should step up and help out. If I write tomorrow, then you will know I made it! If I don't write, then God have mercy on my soul and bless my kids.

<u>TIME IN THE TOWER</u>

November 10, 2004. Wednesday

Well, I made it! It was a blast working the tower. I can see how the Marines get the fever to work up there. We worked two and a half hours in Tower 1. I worked at the tower I always see from my window. It usually gets lots of action. They killed a couple of folks on that tower on Nov 6th. The bad guys were in the field with a weapon. We were only 50 meters from the road outside the base.

In front of the tower was a field with palm trees about 100–150 meters deep.

Then, about 300 meters to the left of the tower was the mosque. It's the tall, skinny tower with a blue roof.

To the left and right of the tower about 150 meters away were some buildings.

Beyond the mosque is the Kendari Market. My tower was on Michigan Avenue, which runs north of the base. To my left was Market Avenue and to the south was Mobile Avenue. We saw lots of people walking down the road and around the buildings. We had a spotting scope and two M240 Bravos, 7.62mm chain-fed machine guns.

A few times, cars and trucks would go down Michigan Avenue, so we would get down and sight our GAUs on them. A GAU can best be described as an M-16 with a collapsible stock. It is shorter than an M-16, so it is easier to get into and out of vehicles and maneuver in tight spaces, like a tower. There was a dirt road on the other side of the field with palm trees about 200 meters away. Cars traveled that road a lot. There was a blue van that stopped in front of our tower. One guy wearing a man-dress got out of the driver's side and walked around the front of the van and looked at us. The Navy JAG watched the man with the spotting scope while giving me details of their actions while I aimed my M240 machine gun at the van. After watching us for a few seconds, the guys in the van flipped us off, he got back in the van, and they drove away. Sometimes I think they stop in front of the tower to see how we will respond. There were plenty of places in the buildings and apartments for Iraqis to hide and take a shot at us. In one of the photos you can see the apartment buildings that overlook the prison walls.

The tower was 6' x 6' and had a steel top. There were sandbags on the sides. The opening in the sandbags in the front and left side was four feet tall and six feet across to allow for easy viewing. It was a rush scoping people out and looking for hostile acts. We saw people herding sheep down a trail, kids playing, people walking, cars and taxis driving around.

I found out this morning that we had eight mortars hit around the base about 11 am. One landed inside the base. I was in the dining facility when they landed, so I never heard the siren sound. The dining facility isn't the place you want to be during a mortar attack. It is just a tin roof building.

Oh, today, in the tower, I was able to get a good look at the mosque that I can see from my room. I learned that the reason I can hear ole Mohammad chanting so well at night is because there are four large PA type speakers on the outside of the mosque that face my room. The mosque is literally across the street from Abu Ghraib. It is a cool purple and gold color with diamond-like designs. The top has a metal crescent moon. It is like a lighthouse tower but no light at the top and no glass. The bottom is like a regular building. We are told that the Iraqis store a lot of weapons inside the mosque because the coalition forces aren't allowed inside. We are able to check inside the mosque by sending the Iraqi National Guard in there to inspect. There was an explosion near the mosque while we were in the tower.

Well, today was the most exciting two and a half hours I've had since I've been here. It is an adrenaline rush to be the only two people in the tower, the first line of defense for the base. The Marines came back and asked if we had been shot at. We said "no." They seemed kind of disappointed. Can you imagine if the Iraqis or anyone on base knew that two attorneys were the front line of defense for two hours?

Oh, I almost forgot…while in the tower we saw about 300 meters out in front of the tower, on the far side of the field with the palm trees, seven men digging a hole on the side of the road. Well, one was digging and six were standing around. Not much different than you would see on a work site back home. They could have been innocently digging a hole to plant a bush or tree, but it was near the road where U.S. soldiers travel, so I was not taking any chances. We radioed the report into the base operations center. The base sent a patrol out to find the men, but before they could get to the location, three of the men got into a land cruiser and left the area. We lost visual on the other four men. I guess they decided not to plant that tree or bush after all. There were houses back there and trails leading up through the woods. We called in lots of action while in the tower. The base operations center even came on the radio and said, "Tower 1, you are doing a great job." Luckily, they didn't add "for attorneys." The other folks in my office thought we were crazy for volunteering to work in the tower, but I'd do it again. I find it hard to stand too long in one spot because I don't want anyone to take a shot at me. Since I won't be able to go deer hunting this year, that is the closest I'll get to being in a deer stand and "hunting." I thought it was great that the Marines told us to call the base operations center before we fire the M240 to shoot anything, but we didn't have to call them before firing our M-16s.

DRESSING DOWN

November 12, 2004. Friday

    Well, today was Friday. My day off, but I never really get a day off. I did sleep one hour later and then went to the gym and then to the office. Today, I did something I have never done in my nine years in the AF. I had to "dress down" a junior officer. My office is trying to develop a dependable way to get files to Camp Victory each week. The Captain who is in charge of assigning Humvees for the base has been telling me for a week he was working on getting us a Humvee. He told Lt. Faulkner, the Navy JAG in my office, yesterday that he was getting us five trucks. But then he double-talks and says he doesn't know if he can get us any trucks. Last night he told Lt. Faulkner that he can give us one after the battery is replaced. Lt. Faulkner told him that his major (me) is going to his office tomorrow and is going to want a truck. The Captain said, "Well, I'll tell your major the same as I tell lieutenant colonels and everyone else…those are my trucks. I've chewed them all out." Well, I didn't learn of the Captain's statement until sometime later. This morning I went to the Captain's office with Lt. Faulkner and I told the Captain I was here to sign for a truck. He said he didn't have any. I said, "You have been working on it for a week."

    He replied, "You can have the one after the battery is replaced." I asked him to let me sign for it now. He declined because it isn't fixed.

I told him that it was no different if I already had this truck and it needed a battery. He then started double-talking.

He said well, "I don't know which ones I am going to give you until I get them all in." That is when I jumped down his throat. I told him I was tired of all this B.S. and his double-talk. He started griping back.

I got in his face and told him, "At ease," and "As you were," to get him to be quiet so I could finish giving him an earful. I got him to shut up and told him all he does is double-talk and he is a liar. I told him I was through with him and I would take it up with the base commander, Colonel Thomas. I went to the base commander's office, but he was out.

I went back to the Captain's office and the Captain said, "Sir, I don't appreciate you coming into my office. ..." I cut him off and told him I didn't give a sh!t about what he did or didn't appreciate. I told him he has no integrity and he was a liar with a severe character deficiency and I was finished with him.

He said, "Yes, sir" and I started leaving. I stepped out the back and yelled for Lt. Faulkner to go. Lt. Faulkner had stepped outside when he heard me jump on the Captain the first time. I went back an hour later and told Colonel Thomas what happened and how I felt about the Captain. The Captain walked into the Colonel's office and the Colonel told him he had to get the lawyers trucks because we needed them to carry the files to the court. The Colonel asked when I had to go on the next convoy, and I said Tuesday. The Colonel said we would have a truck by then. The Captain is about 40-45 years old and a reservist. I bet he's a used car salesman. He just made me mad about lying. Lt. Faulkner said he had never seen a major chew a captain's ass like that before. I just can't stand to be lied to. It takes a lot to make me mad, but this captain did it.

Anyway, I left work at about 2 pm and went to the Morale Welfare and Recreation (MWR) room and watched the movies *American Wedding* and *Fright Night*. I went to the internet café to type an email to my wife, but the computer was missing about six keys. I couldn't think of enough words that didn't require those six letters, so I left to go eat. It was MSgt Brown's birthday. The DFAC made him a birthday cake.

I went back to the office and called home. My son was there because he was getting pink eye. I got to talk to him. I miss him! I talked to my wife and then my parents for a second time, but my time was running out. We are only allowed 15 minutes per phone call. Mom and Dad are at my house in Oklahoma and going with my wife to help her set up for a jewelry expo on Saturday. My wife makes jewelry. Then, Sunday my parents were heading to Shamrock, Texas to visit my aunt. I will call home Sunday night and talk to my daughter.

This job is fun and exciting but being away from the family takes a lot of the fun away. I think I have about 14 more weeks. My son is the only one I'm really worried about because he is so young, and I don't want him to think I'm not coming back. Of course, you miss your children when you are on a business trip for a week but, when your business trip is to a combat zone for several months, you not only miss your children, but when they are young, you wonder if they will remember you if you don't return. You hear news stories or see movies where a person's parent dies when the person is young. The person has few, if any, memories of their parent. That is so sad. Of course, when you talk to your family on the phone, you want to be upbeat and not sad. It is a struggle to hold back your emotions when you hear the sweet, innocent voice of a seven-year-old. Even the moodiness in the voice of my teenage daughter brings a smile to my face.

On the way to the dining hall today, two medivacs flew in. A guy told me that half a mile away from the base a convoy was hit with small arms fire and an RPG. An IED went off at the corner of Market Street and Michigan Avenue at the Kandahar Market. That is the corner that I watched when I was in the tower. It is the corner right past the mosque. It is common for the IEDs to be hidden in dead animals or trash laying on the side of the road. The bad guys wait for a convoy to drive by, or better yet to stop at an intersection. Then, they detonate the IED with wires or remote control, often a cell phone. Despite scanning the roads for possible IEDs, you can't always avoid passing dead animals or trash on the road. You just don't know which ones may explode.

November 14, Sunday

It has been a long two days. Colonel Phelps and General Miller flew in about 6:40 pm Saturday night. They were going to go eat but we had already eaten, so the Colonel told us to come to have a cup of coffee with them. I drank four cups of coffee because I knew it was going to be a long day. I also knew I better drink the coffee inside the dining facility if I wanted to avoid sandy coffee. The Colonel, General, the guys in the Magistrate Cell office, and others walked around the fence line by the detainees who would stop us and tell the General their complaints. About 11:45 pm, Colonel Phelps came back and talked to us and then we left. He invited us to breakfast at 6 am. Of course, I couldn't fall asleep until after 1 am. I had a meeting at 9 am with the General and the interrogators. Then, the Colonel and the General left the base about 11 am. I cut everyone in my office loose at 2:30 pm. I had about 80 files to review and there were no cases for them to work on until I finished. Next Saturday night, the Colonel wants me and others to walk with the General to talk to the detainees about the complaints they may have.

MORE DEATHS

I don't know if I mentioned this earlier, but on Thursday night or Friday night, a KBR employee was about half a mile from Abu in a Humvee that got hit with an RPG. It blew his head off and another guy lost the back of his head. They say you could see down into his stomach. I went to the doctor Saturday to get my flu shot and some sinus medicine for the headache I have had for about two weeks. He asked me if I wanted to see the body without the head. I told him I would pass. We also had a 20-year-old Marine commit suicide. Then, today, a mortar went off and got one Marine in the neck with shrapnel. We heard the explosion at about 2 pm.

On Friday night, we watched tracer rounds being fired from Tower 8 into the apartments that overlook the walls. It was wild. The alarm went off and we manned our positions. Tonight about 7 pm, the alarm went off again when a mortar exploded. It shook our building. They said it was outside the base, but it was loud. It might have been a VBIED, also known as a car bomb. I believe Ramadan is over next Tuesday. Maybe it will calm down then. They have a few more days of fighting in Fallujah. They have the roads blocked to keep the bad guys from leaving, but they still do. Since Abu is only about 12 miles away from Fallujah, and on the way out, they come by and shoot mortars at us. It's been really active lately. The Colonel wants us to get out to the field, so we need to schedule trips to Mosul and Tikrit soon. We can chopper out there...I hope. The Colonel did buy us a case of non-alcoholic St. Pauli Girl beer with his own money. He sent it when our guys came back the other day in the convoy. It's getting cooler. Eighty degrees during the day and around 60 at night. I may start showering at night to stay out of the morning cold air. It's chilly walking across the parking lot to the shower and coming back half wet.

November 16, 2004. Tuesday

Found this pen downstairs. Good pens are a hot commodity. Last night was interesting. As usual over the past few days, we got mortared twice and a firefight started at 8 pm. We watched it last night from the window in the dayroom in our living quarters. You could see the red tracer rounds fly across the sky from Tower 8 to the apartments. Tower 8 is two towers away from the one I guarded. Tower 8 is only about 100 to 150 yards from my window. I was planning on bringing the camera home tonight and filming and taking photos of the firefight. But it is 9:15 pm and there has been no action.

CHANGES IN THE OFFICE

Managing the office has gotten busier lately. I have to find people to go on the convoy Friday to take the case files to Camp Victory. We had 109 cases ready from Monday, plus the 39 I did today. That's already three boxes full and the Magistrate Cell told us we should expect an average of 75 a day for three weeks. Most are the people captured in Falluja. Then, I have to find people to go to the combat lifesavers course near the Baghdad International Airport (BIAP), which is three days, then people for the advance party to go to Camp Bucca to set up our office. The plan is to move our office to Bucca in December. Bucca is a prison compound way down in southern Iraq and is supposed to be safer. I have to select people to go around with the General on Saturday night when he walks and talks to the detainees, then I have to pick three people for the video home taping project and get three of the attorneys to schedule trips to Falluja, Tikrit, and Mosul in the next couple of weeks, then tell Colonel Phelps how I can use two Navy Master of Arms investigators (which I don't want) because they have bad attitudes.

Then I have to move the NIPR computer to a neutral location so everyone can share it. It's gotten so bad that the first thing in the morning, everyone draws a number from a hat to see who goes first, second, etc. It is the only computer you can send emails home from. I don't participate in the name drawing. I tell them I will get on there, anytime.

I do work on the NIPR computer, too. We have a competition with a computer game called Pocket Tanks. We made brackets for a tournament. Lt. Hayes Larsen, a Navy JAG in my office, started an underground newsletter called the Abu Gazette. It is just a joke about life in our office. It is pretty funny.

We have killer flies here. They are everywhere, and they attack your face. I just finally killed one when it landed on my neck. Isn't that crazy? I killed another one with a towel. I put a fly-ribbon-sticky-thing up in the office because the fly kept getting me. I hung it from the ceiling, right above my head where I sit at my desk. It still took two days to catch that dang thing. Today, another one landed on the weight on the bottom of the ribbon where it wasn't sticky. Crazy bugs!

We just finished watching an animated movie called the *Incredibles*. One of the guys bought it from a local Iraqi vendor today for $2. It isn't even out on DVD and he bought it on DVD. Someone filmed it from inside a movie theater. During the movie, two people stood up and walked past the camera. It was funny. What do you expect for $2?

What else is going on? JAX, the assignment office for AF JAGs, finally received my JAG bonus contract that I sent one month ago. Maybe I'll get paid for my bonus soon. To receive the money you have to commit to more time in the Air Force. Otherwise, after your four years, you can leave anytime with a six-months prior notice.

NATURE NIGHT CALLS

Let me tell you, life here can be pretty crazy sometimes. Most of us keep empty water bottles by our bed to pee in at night, so you don't have to get dressed, put on your bullet proof vest, and helmet and carry your weapon just to go to the port-a-potties. I've never had to pee so much in my life. I also keep a couple of bottles to brush my teeth in my room. I spit in an empty bottle and rinse with a bottle of water. Sometimes I'll go and brush my teeth at the water buffalo and spit on the rocks. Otherwise, I have to put on my body armor and vest and walk about 20 yards to the shower shed to brush my teeth! Crazy huh?

SMALL WORLD

Today I learned that Lt. Larson went to law school with Capt. Kenneth Imo who is assigned to my office back home. They knew each other at Wake Forrest. Small world. I shaved my head while here and sent a photo to Capt. Imo. Before I left, he tried to convince me to surrender to my receding hairline and shave my head. I told him not everyone looks good bald, and he is the exception to the rule. He wears a bald head well, but he is a 6' tall former college football player. I'm a skinny white guy with glasses. I figured if I wanted to see if I could pull it off, then now would be the time. I probably already wrote about it but when we went to Camp Victory a few weeks ago to talk to the attorney about how to collect evidence, one of the attorneys was one year ahead of me in law school, and his best friend was a law school classmate of mine. They were all from Arkansas and part of the First Calvary division. The guy also used to be partners with Chris Hayes who is an attorney in my hometown in Arkansas. I also learned that one of the guys who works in the Magistrate Cell next door to my office lives and works in Fayetteville. He is a partner at Basset law firm where one of my law school classmates works. Small world! Well, it's almost 10 pm and I need to get to sleep. Nothing else to do, really.

November 17, 2004. Wednesday

Well, a long day today. The Colonel and General came in today at 3 pm in a convoy, but the chopper didn't arrive until 3:40 pm. We talked about a lot of issues. He asked, "Hugh, have I ever told you this place is a sh!thole?"

To which I replied, "Yes, sir, every Saturday night you visit." He also said our Humvee (that I was finally able to obtain) was a piece of crap and we shouldn't put it in a convoy. You don't want one that is likely to break down outside the wire nor one that has a cloth top. He talked to Colonel Thomas, the base commander, about getting us a better one. I'm going to the embassy Saturday or Sunday to have a meeting with Colonel Phelps and Lt. Colonel McLaughlin about policy. Lt. Colonel McLaughlin is the Army JAG in charge of the third step in the process, e.g. prosecution. The embassy sent back files because they didn't have photos. Well, if there were photos taken, then my group gets them before we forward the files. Besides, when the embassy calls and talks to the witnesses, they can ask the witness to bring any photos they have. They also want us to send all the detainees who were captured all at once, as a group of files. The problem is some are kept on military intelligence hold longer than others because they are being interrogated. So, it's ridiculous to hold up five files while waiting on the sixth guy. Besides, not all of them will be prosecuted.

The hospital beside our office is used to treat the detainees. As you can imagine, most of the detainees were captured by U.S. soldiers somewhere in Iraq after some type of violent engagement, such as a gunfight, car explosion, or assault. The detainees sometime arrive with bullet wounds and other injuries and the U.S. military physicians treat the detainees. It is a large facility with dozens of inpatient beds. We have a lot of Iraqis in the hospital who were brought in from the recent battle at Fallujah. They don't have any information with them, so we don't know if they were innocent bystanders who were injured or came from the Fallujah hospital because of a car wreck. It's not like the bad guys wear a uniform. So, unless the soldiers in the field bring statements with the detainees, then we don't have any reason to call them a detainee and we can't keep them. If we call them a detainee, then they have to go all the way through the process: the Mag Cell determining whether there is probable cause to detain them; me reviewing the evidence to determine whether they should be reviewed by the Combined Review and Release Board who in turn determines if they are a threat to coalition forces; or my staff writing prosecution memos and the embassy attorneys prosecuting the detainee. Of course, the MPs and Marines aren't happy with that, but we have to have a reason to keep them. The guys in the Magistrate Cell will have to look at all the information available and determine whether there is probable cause to detain them.

VISITING SADDAM

Colonel Phelps told us he visited Saddam Hussein and he was looking good. He is in a secret location in Iraq, but I'm guessing BIAP or Camp Cropper. Colonel Phelps would only tell us that he is in a "place made for one" and it has "adequate facilities." Saddam will be tried in an Iraqi court by the Iraqi people because that is who he mistreated and abused. He shouldn't be tried in an international court because where was the international community when he was torturing people and issuing death sentences? All the international community did was to say, "He shouldn't do that."

CLIENTS IN THE DESERT

I saw a girl today who came in for legal advice on a personal issue. She was upset because her husband wanted a divorce and was taking their two-year-old daughter to his mom's house about two hours away from where she lived. My client (the wife) didn't know how to contact her daughter or mother-in-law. He also took her son (not his biological son) to her mother's house. What a mess. I'm trying to contact a Florida military base and put her in contact with an Army JAG because she is in the Army. They will be in a much better position to help her.

I didn't get home until after 9 pm. Long day. Head hurts. Oh, yesterday the explosions were four mortars that hit the southeast part of the base.

We learned today that a map of Abu was found on an Iraqi which had the dining facility and other areas marked as targets. They still haven't found the Russian jammer which someone has on the base and it is interfering with our global positioning equipment. A satellite picked it up and contacted the base and asked if we knew about it. We didn't! They think it is mobile, so probably on a port-a-potty truck. Today was my gym day but I couldn't make it. I'll try tomorrow night.

TRAVEL TIME

November 19, 2004. Friday

Well, usual day, worked files. No mortars attack today. Going to try and catch a ride on a convoy tomorrow to go to BIAP and then catch the Rhino to the embassy. The Rhino is an RV made of armor. The road from BIAP to the embassy is the most dangerous. The route called Route Irish is the worst! It takes about 20 minutes to get to BIAP from Abu, then, and about 40 minutes to get to the embassy. I'm meeting Lt. Colonel McLaughlin who is the deputy SJA and OIC of the embassy legal office and Colonel Phelps who is the SJA. We have to talk and get on the same page regarding what the case files need as evidence.

I'm sending two people to get M1114 Humvee training tomorrow, so they will be qualified to drive the vehicle. Then they can pick me up Monday at BIAP. We needed to take files to Camp Victory and get supplies, so the timing is perfect for them to pick me up. Of course, this is assuming we can borrow a Humvee to drive. From the palace (embassy) I'll have to hitchhike or catch a Rhino to BIAP on Monday.

We watched *Carlito's Way* tonight. It is an old movie with Al Pacino. I've seen it many times and it is still good. Kind of sad but set in the 70s in New York. It made me miss my wife. It has the song, "You Are So Beautiful" which reminded me of her. I met my wife when I was in 10th grade. I first saw her at a swimmer's club when a mutual friend introduced us. I asked her out that very moment and knew from the first date I was going to marry her. We got married while in college and shortly thereafter started a family. It was hard but a privilege to support a wife and baby while finishing college and law school. I had goals that I wanted to achieve, which included becoming a husband, father, and attorney. Being impatient, I wanted to achieve them all within a short time. I don't recommend it, but it is possible.

TRAVELING NERVES

For some reason, the last couple of days I have been getting worried about traveling. I've just got this weird feeling. I try to remember Matthew 6:27 and 6:34, in which Jesus says, "Can any of you add one cubit to his height by worrying?" and "Don't worry about tomorrow because tomorrow will worry about itself. Each day has enough trouble of its own." Sometimes, I feel like I don't care if I get killed, but then I think about my kids and my high school sweetheart, now my wife, and I want to spend more time with them. I think the "I don't care" attitude is more accurately described as I am at peace if I am killed. I've written goodbye letters to my family telling them how much I love them, and I have taken steps to ensure they will be provided for financially. What else can you do? It is important not to be distracted with thoughts of home or worry of dying while you are in a combat zone. Before you get there, you have to make peace with knowing you may not come back and be okay with it. We can take every precaution to be safe, but we can't be fooled into believing we can control every situation, especially in a combat zone. Make your peace and go do your job.

I did get a care package from my office back home today. Fudge, papers, envelopes, Santa hat, and little stockings, and much needed deodorizers. I wrote a thank you letter and asked MSgt. Brown to mail it for me. Well, I'm going to put new batteries in the camera so I can take pictures at the embassy and if the "Good Lord willing and the creek don't rise," I'll be writing more Monday when I get back.

November 22, 2004. Monday

Well, I made it back! I left Abu by walking out to the line of trucks to catch a ride on the convoy. A truck pulled up and asked me if I needed a ride. I said, "Yes," and threw my stuff in the back seat of the Hummer. Then I looked up and said, "This is a soft-top truck…I'm not riding in here." I grabbed my stuff and got in an M1114 which is the best armored Humvee. The guy in the soft top truck said that I should go with my gut, to which I replied, "My gut is telling me not to ride in a soft top!"

It took about 20 minutes to get to BIAP. Airman Trussel picked me up at the clearing barrel and took me to BIAP. I waited for the Rhino to leave at 10:45 am to take me to the embassy palace. As soon as the Rhino left, we turned around because they closed Route Irish due to a VBIED exploding. They called a chopper to pick me up and said it would be 15 minutes. Two hours later the chopper hadn't arrived. They said it had mechanical problems. By that time, the road opened, so we got on the Rhino and left for the embassy across town. I didn't have breakfast or lunch and got there at about 3:30 pm. I took pictures of the embassy. I showed the people at the embassy office pictures of Abu and they freaked out. They had no idea how bad it was.

GOING TO COURT AGAIN

The next morning, I went to court. It was an interesting ride through the red zone, which is the dangerous area of the city. I took pictures. Colonel Phelps and I rode in the second truck. We had a gun truck in front and rear and a white suburban that keeps people from getting beside us. We have to watch for civilian cars getting too close because they could explode. At one point during the trip, a car driven by an Iraqi was trying to get in between our trucks, so a U.S. civilian soldier leaned out the back door of the white suburban and pointed a rifle at the Iraqi driver. The Iraqi driver finally got the message. Before we left, they briefed us that six Blackwater guys, the private contractors who act as security details, had been killed earlier that morning. I watched two hearings in the Iraqi judge's chambers at the Central Criminal Court of Iraq. At the preliminary hearing, which is held to decide if there is enough to proceed with prosecuting the case, the Iraqi judges won't start before 10:30 am. The judge sits at this desk and there are four chairs in front, two on each side facing each other. The witness sits in one chair and the Iraqi defense attorney (paid for by the Iraqi government) sits beside the witness. The interpreter sits across from the witness and a JAG from the embassy legal office sits across from the Iraqi defense attorney. A court reporter sits at the corner of the judge's desk and handwrites everything on carbon paper so we can have a copy. The defense attorney never says anything, though he may write a few words.

People walk in during the hearing. Each witness was interrupted by five people. People just come in and start talking to the judge in the middle of the hearing. The judge walks around and talks to the people who walk in while the witness is testifying. It's the craziest thing. The detainee sits in the corner and is watched by one of our MPs who looks like he is about to fall asleep because he has been up since 4 am. It is comical. The bathroom at the courthouse is nasty. I took pictures. It has three little rooms like stalls. There is a hole in the floor with ceramic around it. You squat over it and then take a little water hose to wash it down and to wash yourself. No toilet paper anywhere to be found.

When we were leaving the courthouse, the military security team surrounded us and walked us to the trucks. There was a kid about 10 years old hanging around the security team and the team says the kid always tells them he wants to kill them and that his dad is a terrorist.

We left the courthouse and Colonel Phelps and I went to the convention center beside the Al Rasheed hotel that was on TV after being bombed. The Combined Review and Release Board is in the convention center. There were four Iraqis on the board. Amazingly, the Iraqi board members have to lie about where they work or they will get killed. Can you imagine not being able to tell your friends and some of your family where you work? The Iraqi board members have to be careful because they could be killed if the insurgents, anti-coalition forces, terrorists, or Al Qaeda learn they are working with the U.S. If the bad guys got mad enough to shoot at the driver of the port-a-potty truck, just imagine how they would feel about a board member. There's something to be said about those who are willing to risk their lives to improve their country.

We had lunch at the hotel and walked around the shops.

Colonel Phelps, Lt. Colonel McLaughlin, and I sat down Saturday night at the embassy and talked about policy and how to handle the cases. Together we are the three heads of the process; well Col Phelps is the head of all the processes. It was very productive and I did learn that one of the interpreters at the embassy legal office from California quit. She wouldn't go to court because she was scared. The female interpreter from Iraq that works at the embassy legal office may be fired. Her dad works at the embassy but was just fired for having ties to terrorists and taking documents from the embassy. The polygraphers were there to give her a polygraph test.

When I arrived back at Camp Victory, we rode around Uday and Quasay Hussein's bombed-out palaces, which sit beside each other on the lake called Lost Lake. This is a different lake than the one where the embassy and the Camp Victory legal office sit. The sons' palaces are about a one-minute drive from the Camp Victory legal office. They found a lot of bodies in Lost Lake because one of the sons would go out and pick up prostitutes and bring them home. He would then kill them and throw their bodies in the lake. Rumor is the #1 (Saddam) is kept in the bombed-out palaces. I doubt it.

I made it back and it is cold tonight. The wind is blowing through my cardboard window here at Abu Ghraib and it is making the sheet I use as a curtain wave through the air.

Tomorrow is my dad and sister's birthday. That is #4 and #5 birthdays I have missed.

BACK TO PRISON

November 28, 2004. Sunday

Well, I haven't written in a while, just in a mood to keep pressing on. It feels like holding your breath and wishing time would go by fast, like the time before and after ripping off the band aid. I don't want to think about home or family or have any emotion. I don't want to feel. I just want to do my job, make good decisions that will keep myself and my staff safe, and focus on one minute at a time. Thinking about home can leave you distracted and sad and make you a liability.

Did find out about the mortar attack last Sunday… four of our guys went to drop off their laundry at the hooch (our living quarters) about 10 am. There was a water truck blocking the road, so Lt. Larsen, who was driving the Humvee, decided not to wait and went around it by driving around the far side of the building and parked on the backside. Three of the guys waited under a concrete hang (outside door frame) that is attached to the building of our living quarters, while Staff Sergeant Jesse Bascomb, aka Jesse the Body, (an Air Force paralegal in our office who received the nickname because he went to the gym often) used the port-a-potty 10 feet away.

Bang! A mortar landed about 50 feet away from the port-a-potty, right where we always park the Humvee and would have parked had Lt. Larsen waited on the water truck to move. The mortar destroyed a truck that was parked there and the water buffalo that sits about 50 feet from the door of our living area. Jesse ran out of the port-a-potty while trying to pull up his pants. I bet it scared the crap out of him [pun intended]. They ran into the concrete room attached to the concrete hang where the guys were standing, and then three more mortars landed. I got pictures of the aftermath.

They all believe in divine intervention because I am the one who always drives the Humvee and I never park on the backside. Staff Sergeant Bascombe drives when I'm gone and this time, he decided to ask Lt. Larsen to drive. Lt. Larsen wanted to go through a mud hole instead of waiting on the water truck to move. The mortar hit right where we all walk every day.

Thanksgiving was nice. I had to wait an hour in line but it was worth it. The General was there and shook our hands. He remembered my name as Hugh, but I don't know why. This is probably why he is a two-star general.

We had a Washington Post reporter fly in with the General on Friday...no interactions really. Saturday, the General came by the office after we all just walked out about 9:30 pm. Luckily MSgt. Brown was still there to say hi. The General only stayed about 30 seconds.

Today, I was sitting at my desk at the office sewing my insulated shirt that had ripped under the arms. All of a sudden, I hear, "Room, attention!" Then General Miller walked into our office and went straight to my office and pushed open the door. There I am with a needle and thread. I said, "Hello, sir. You caught me sewing." He replied with a laugh, "Good, Hugh. A diversified lawyer."

He asked how things were going and what he could do to make it better. I told him about our trip planned to Mosul tomorrow night and to Tikrit on Dec 9th. He was pleased we were getting to the field to train people on how to collect evidence. I told him how we have a plan to get the physical evidence, e.g. weapons seized, to court and he said that it was going to be a mess. I told him we are going to see if it increases the sentences any by dropping four RPG grenade launchers on the judge's desk in court. If not, we won't' do it. I just wanted to try a new approach. He was pleased. He said he had one more week and then was going to the Pentagon to be the Deputy Security Officer of all the Army bases. He was picked by the Secretary of Defense. He said it has been a long two years. He had been at Guantanamo Bay before coming to Iraq. He is the world expert on detainees. I told him I saw him on TV in the dining facility last week. It was on *60 minutes* or *20/20* with a reporter interviewing him about Gitmo. He seemed like a great guy and was really approachable.

THE MARINE GRIPES

I did have to gripe at the office staff yesterday. Saturdays are our long days because Colonel Phelps comes in with the General. We have to stay until the General comes by. If the Colonel doesn't come, then I cut people loose about 10 pm. Anyway, Saturday morning, before work, I heard the Marine JAG talking to MSgt. Brown at the living quarters about how it is so unproductive for us to stay late just in case General Miller comes by. So, at the office I called a meeting and said…I didn't want to hear anymore complaining about staying late. We were directed by Colonel Phelps to stay, so we stay. If they think it is so unproductive, then we won't watch a movie Saturday night and we won't play computer games. I told them we would clean weapons and work on files. I told them it is the basic military order to follow commands of superior officers and the enlisted know it as part of their enlistment oath. I said to complain reflects bad character, especially for officers. Then I said I want to see all the officers in my office. I told them to cut it out. Don't gripe in front of junior people or enlisted members. We have to toe the line and lead by example and I expect them to stop the complaints when they hear it.

Then today, the Marine JAG had his head down and was sleeping. I talked to him alone and asked him if he was feeling okay. I told him that I can't have him sleeping during the workday and that the enlisted members in the office are commenting about it. Also, his paralegal, the

Army enlisted member, was trying to sleep, too. I told him I would give him time off if he was exhausted, but he declined. He confessed that the medicine he was just prescribed makes him sleepy. I recommended he talk to the doctor about taking it at night. Then he was worried about showing poor officership because of griping and now sleeping. He does a good job but needs to work on image and leading by example. I have to remember that these officers have only been in the military for less than two years, so some need more mentoring. I'm usually laid back, but I've had to step up and do some mentoring lately. I'm learning a lot about leadership and adjusting to it.

I was talking to Lt. Larsen who has been in the Navy for less than one year. I told him it was ok to be friendly with lower-ranking members of the office, but he has to be able to separate himself and make a hard decision such as giving an order to go on a dangerous mission. You always have to be objective and remember you are the leader. Just like I have had to pick people for three trips to different cities in Iraq. I had to decide who was going to take the Hummer on a convoy and some of it was during Ramadan when attacks increase. I had to decide objectively and couldn't be biased. It is harmful to the morale of the office if you don't select someone with whom you are friendly because others will see it as favoritism, even if it isn't. The same is true when I had to pick who would go on the advance team to Bucca and who will get qualified on the M1114 Hummer. It is okay to be friendly to keep morale up and motivate people, but always remember you are the leader.

I am very pleased with the work the office has done. Since October 1st, we have reviewed 1,764 files. I have selected 401 files for prosecution. That's a lot of files. General Miller wants us to send 100 cases for prosecution every month and we have doubled that. General Miller did tell me the average stay at Abu is seven months and out of 9,000 detainees over the whole time, only 50 have come back. So, recidivism is almost non-existent.

Everyone has been clearing out old files that have been sitting and waiting on more evidence. These are files on individual detainees that we have identified as needing more witness statements, photos of the detainee and his weapon and/or explosives, or other information we believe exists. We currently don't have sufficient evidence to make a determination as to whether the detainees should be prosecuted in the Iraqi court or sent to the CRRB for a security risk determination. I set a 14-day limit for our guys to gather more evidence. If we don't get the evidence within that time limit, then we will recommend no prosecution due to the lack of evidence and send the case to the board for a security assessment. There are just too many files to process to sit on them. Also, it isn't fair for the detainee to remain in prison without sufficient evidence to hold them and it isn't fair to the soldiers to not give them another opportunity to provide the evidence. We are in a combat zone, so it's not like the paperwork is being completed and filed in downtown Denver. We don't want to get it wrong and risk the lives of our soldiers who may be harmed by the detainee, but we have to balance it against the detainees' due process rights. Therefore, giving the soldiers another two weeks to provide the needed evidence seems to be the right balance of everyone's interest.

I'm planning on going to Tikrit on December 9th. I decided not to go to Mosul because it would have been too many people from our office going. I selected Lt. Larson and "Tech" Shane Thomas, an Air Force paralegal, because it is the area of the country where their cases come from. Staff Sergeant Bascombe wants to go, even after surviving his near port-a-potty death. He is not partnered with an attorney, so he helps Lt. Larson and Tech with their cases. Staff Sergeant Bascombe will be assigned to work those cases when Tech and Lt. Larsen go with the advance team to set up our office in Bucca. I'm letting MSgt. Brown go as an office leader to let him get out of here for awhile. He will be a great representative of the office leadership. We must build a strong rapport with the U.S. soldiers and investigators in that region of Iraq, so they understand that we need them to provide us with better evidence to prosecute cases. Otherwise, we have to turn the detainees loose even if they should be prosecuted. But, without evidence we can't detain them in the first place. The investigators need to know what type of evidence is needed, so they can provide support for their cases.

I know collecting evidence isn't what the soldiers are trained to do. Can you imagine engaging in a fire fight, capturing the individual, and now having to remember to take photos of the guy who just tried to kill you? Not only take photos, but photos of the individual with the weapons used against you, and, oh yea, write a witness statement under oath about what happened. And, transport the detainee and paperwork to Abu. These aren't our rules. These are the rules set by the Iraqi judges who will ultimately decide if there is sufficient evidence to send the detainee to prison or set the detainee free to possibly go fight our soldiers again. Staying alive is no longer enough. The soldiers are now performing duties as witnesses to a crime and criminal investigators. It is like no other war in the past.

THE BAD GUYS

Friday, I walked around Camp Redemption. That is the camp that has the detainees kept inside cyclone fences here on Abu. These are the detainees that my office decides whether to prosecute or not.

We talked to the juveniles in the camp and told them about the status of their cases and how we are trying to get Iraqis to hold hearings for juveniles. The juveniles are scared that if the Iraqis have them in custody, then the Iraqis will beat them. We told them we are talking about turning them over to the Iraq Ministry of Labor. The juveniles thought that meant they would be given shovels and have to work because it is "labor." Funny, huh? We told them because of all the recent attacks it is too dangerous for them to have outside visitors. They asked that if it is so dangerous then why do we have them living in tents? Right after they said that a mortar dropped, and we ran to the bunker. The Iraqi juveniles asked, "If y'all are scared then why come out here?" That could have been a question asked to the leaders of all the countries that sent troops to Iraq. The easy answer for military members is, "Because it's my job." I guess they don't appreciate that we are visiting them to let them know we are working on their cases as quickly as possible and to answer any questions they have about their status.

There was a 10-year-old boy in detention who admitted to throwing 10–15 grenades at U.S. troops. The detainees are housed in a fenced area, like a cyclone fence with concertina wire on top. There are approximately 20 juveniles in each fenced section. Some of the detainees are probably innocent and were just rounded up for being in the wrong place at the wrong time. Some will kill you if given the chance. Dealing with juveniles in the U.S. pales in comparison to dealing with juveniles in an Iraq prison. The conundrum is what do you do with these juveniles that you can barely identify. There are no parents demanding the release of their children. A child soldier is a foreign concept to Americans. We couldn't imagine training 10-year-old Timmy to throw grenades at other people. The fact that Americans tend to think of children as innocent is what makes a child soldier a real threat to U.S. soldiers. It is no secret that child soldiers have been and continue to be used in different countries. Since the 1990s, thousands of Iraqi boys as young as 10 years old have attended "boot camps" to learn to shoot weapons and be indoctrinated into political thinking. Therefore, the children who have been detained by U.S. soldiers are there because they attempted to or did, in fact, harm coalition forces. It is important to recognize these aren't children who shoplifted candy at the store. These are "children" who have been trained to kill and use their age to their advantage. Failure to put the situation into perspective and see this through the lens of life in Iraq and not Kansas can result in dangerous children being placed in a position in which they can harm U.S. soldiers. That doesn't mean they necessarily need lengthy prison sentences but need detention and re-indoctrination before being released. For the time being, we are keeping the children separate from the adults, while the Iraqi government decides what to do with them.

Well, it's time to start in a new journal.

December 6, 2004. Monday

I haven't written in a while because it has been pretty quiet around here. Last week I sent some guys from my office up to Mosul. It was called Nineveh in the Bible and was the town God told Jonah to go to and preach, but Jonah got swallowed by a whale before arriving.

Today I went to BIAP. It was only 10.6 miles from the gates at Abu to the gate at BIAP. We traveled down Routes Mobile and Tampa and then a little down Route Yankee. It is almost 10 minutes due east and 10 minutes due north. Going east, it is a six-lane highway with a median. We pass under three overpasses. The road that runs out front of Abu will take you to Fallujah if you head west. You don't want to get your east and west directions mixed up.

Once you get into the BIAP gate, you drive 14 miles to the Camp Victory legal office at TF (task force) 134, which is on the lake. There isn't much to see on the road to BIAP. Mostly dusty fields, a few shepherds with sheep, some Pepsi roadside stands. I still don't know what those are about. There aren't many cars on the road. We do pass the burned-out Hummer that is about half a mile from Abu which was hit with an RPG and took one guy's head off and another's halfway off.

The vehicle is upside down and all burned up with just a frame left on the side of the road. It happened about four weeks ago.

Inside BIAP we passed by the airport. It was uneventful. There has been a lull in the attacks at Abu and BIAP for the past two weeks. At BIAP, I bought all the women in my life (five) silver pendants for necklaces. I also got my wife and kids' first names and our last name embroidered on name tapes in Arabic. It is priced by weight, so it cost me $40. I bought Christmas lights to have for our Christmas party in our living quarters.

We also brought back Lt. Wall, a Navy JAG, to our Abu office. He wanted to come to Abu to work, so he could be more productive than working at the legal office at Camp Victory.

SADDAM'S HEARING

Oh, I finally got a coffee cup with a lid, I know, about time! I had to buy it a Camp Victory because there weren't any at the store on Abu. Now, I can drink my coffee without having to cover it after each swallow. Just another advantage Camp Victory has over Abu Ghraib—other than heaters and the absence of a barrage of mortars—coffee without sand. Other than that, I walked to the courthouse which was about one block from the legal office at Camp Victory. It is the one that held Saddam's hearing. It is really small…maybe 40 feet square. I sat in the chair Saddam sat in during the hearing and got my picture taken in it. Wow! They also tried one of the soldiers who was involved in the Abu Ghraib prison abuse scandal in this room. Well, I'm tired and I'm going to hang the lights in my room and then read and go to bed.

December 7, 2004. Tuesday

Well, same ole thing…not too busy…waiting on files to come in. We have reviewed 1800 files from Oct 1st to Nov 30th. Today, I reviewed a file on one of the abductors of Nick Berg and who was present during his beheading.

For those who don't remember, Nick Berg was an American freelance radio tower repairman who went to Iraq. He was abducted and beheaded on May 7, 2004, according to a video released on the internet, by Islamist militants in response to the Abu Ghraib prisoner abuse. It has been reported he was beheaded by Abu Musab al-Zarqawi. In case you aren't familiar with Zarqawi, he founded Al Qaeda in Iraq in October 2004, after receiving Osama Bin Laden's endorsement. He is also credited with starting ISIS (Islamic State of Iraq and Syria), which is also known as ISIL (Islamic State of Iraq and the Levant). The U.S. killed Zarqawi in June 2006.

It was this horrific deed that prompted me to buy a knife before I deployed to Iraq and kept it attached to my body every day. In preparation for my deployment, I went to Wal-Mart in Altus, Oklahoma to shop for a knife. It wasn't a typical shopping trip. I asked the employee in the sporting goods department to let me see different knives. As I handled each knife, I envisioned having to fight the employee with that knife. I'm sure he was wondering why I was looking at him funny. After going through that exercise a few times, I finally settled on a knife that had a sheath that allowed for quick release that I could hang on the front of my body armor. I had vowed to die fighting before being taken alive and beheaded.

I also reviewed the file of a guy who was involved in the capture of PFC Jessica Lynch. She was a 19-year-old Army soldier who was captured on March 23, 2003, when her convoy was ambushed. She was knocked unconscious when her vehicle crashed. Out of the three groups in the convoy, eleven soldiers were killed in the attack and five others were captured and rescued 21 days later. She was rescued by U.S. Special Operations Forces on April 1, 2003, when she was found in a hospital. The detainee described the firefight and how he was the one who drove Jessica Lynch to the hospital which was being used as a headquarters. The detainee described that there was a Black American soldier who fought bravely but was killed after he ran out of ammunition. I know the Army briefed the family members about the ambush on the convoy because the circumstances were somewhat of a debacle with some of the trucks getting stuck in the sand, missing the turn in the road, running out of gas, and getting separated, but I often wondered if the families of soldiers who died that day ever learned the details of how brave they were.

PFC Lynch was the only survivor of the five people in her group. Because she was knocked unconscious from the initial explosions, no one is available to tell first-hand how the four other soldiers in her group fought bravely during the 60-to-90-minute engagement. These brave soldiers killed weren't infantry, but clerks, truck drivers, and similar career fields. Just another example of soldiers, regardless of their occupation, giving their all. Hearing a member of the opposing force say how brave the U.S. soldiers were in defending against the ambush is bittersweet.

PRISONERS ESCAPED

Today, we were told that two detainees escaped the tent site (the tents are inside the cyclone fence area). They used poles from the tent to break through the fence and then made it to an area of the camp without a guard tower and climbed out of Abu! So, that tells me if two people can break out during daylight hours, then people can break in! One hundred insurgents broke into a police station nearby and took it over. There is now concern that they may try to break into Abu. They just want to break in, grab a U.S. military officer and get out. Lt. Colonels and above carry their pistols with magazines loaded.

Last Saturday there was a VBIED (Vehicle Borne Improvised Explosive Device), or what civilians may call a car bomb, during the CRRB (Combined Review and Release Board) which is held at the convention center right beside the Al Rasheed Hotel. It was one of the first places I visited when I arrived in Baghdad and watched the board review over 100 files to determine whether each of the detainees was a security risk or should be released. The car exploded in the red zone near the checkpoint. It destroyed about 25 cars. Colonel Phelps got permission to walk one of the Iraqi board members to his car in the red zone. When they got there the board member's car had been blown up and was upside down on top of another car. Body parts were lying around. Before they got back to the convention center the news was already on CNN. A lot of reporters live in the Al Rasheed Hotel. My paralegal from back home was in the parking lot during the explosion and ended up with a bloody nose.

I'm getting ready to chopper to Tikrit on Thursday to brief the troops on how to collect better evidence, so we can be more successful when prosecuting detainees. We did catch #49 on the deck of cards of the most wanted the other day but I haven't seen him in my file, yet. Number 49 is Husam Muhammad Amin, head of National Monitoring Directorate, and reportedly captured April 27, 2003, and released 2005. Due to his high intelligence value, he would be kept near BIAP and would not make it to Abu. He was part of Saddam's inner circle and served as Iraq's liaison with the United Nations' weapons inspectors. In his position, he would have knowledge of weapons of mass destruction, and he refused to allow the U.N. inspectors access to the palaces or other sensitive sites to search for weapons of mass destruction.

FLYING AND DYING

December 10, 2004. Friday

    I flew to Tikrit Thursday morning at about 8 am. It was an hour-long via Black Hawk helicopter. I sat facing forward on the helicopter's left side. About 15 minutes into the flight, the door gunner on my side shot about 25 rounds into four guys standing in a dirt field after we passed them. I saw the guys standing there as we flew over them which seemed about 50 feet high. I was facing the front of the helicopter, so I couldn't see them after we flew over. I looked at a Lt. Colonel who was facing backward and he gave me a thumbs-up sign and waved goodbye. I asked if we got them and he tapped his right arm in about four places going up against his arm. Apparently, those four guys fired small weapons at us. We flew so low we had to rise to go over power lines. It was fun, but a cold flight.

    Tikrit is North of Baghdad between Mosul and Samarra. It is the birthplace of Saddam. The Tigris River flows through the palace area. From one picture you can see the Tigris and in the field behind me is where they found Saddam hiding in a hole.

It is also the area where a rocket took down a helicopter about one year ago killing the Army's Command Sergeant Major (who was also an Army paralegal) on November 7, 2003, near Tikrit. From that view, you can see the north part of the city of Tikrit. They said the church there by the palace is the oldest Christian church existing since Mesopotamia. Uday, Saddam's son, known for his sexual crimes, had a palace there. We dropped a bomb on it but it was still standing. There is a public highway running through the palace grounds. Kind of crazy, but we put a cyclone fence up around it and tarps so people on the highway can't see what is on either side. There is a bridge over the Tigris River. First time I've seen green grass and hills since I've been in Iraq. I enjoyed the trip and the views. It was very cold, colder than Abu. They had nice port-a-potties in Tikrit. We called them Cadillacs because they had sinks built in. They were not as nice as the gold toilets at the embassy but a lot better than the ones at Abu, which tend to be pockmarked from mortars. Anyway, I was excited to get back to the old Iraqi prison, even if it only had regular looking port-a-potties.

December 15, 2004. Wednesday

I'm back in Abu. It is my first real whole day off. It was great. I slept from 6:30 pm till 8:30 am the next day... 14 hours! I got up and watched the movie *Alamo*, went to the gym, then showered, came back, and watched *Sleepy Hollow*. Tonight I watched *Ocean's 11* and then *Ocean's 12*. *Ocean's 12* isn't on DVD yet but one of the guys bought it from a local vendor. It has been dropping to about 17 degrees at night and slowly warming during the day. Still no heaters! Just one heater in the dayroom of our living area that goes out often. Then a couple of rooms up here in our living quarters have one. My hooch is cold. I had to re-tape my window because the cardboard was falling off. My sleeping bag keeps me warm when I'm sleeping but otherwise it is cold!

MAKING PLANS FOR THE HOLIDAYS

December 16, 2004. Thursday

Well, I had 200 files waiting on me to review when I got into work today. Then about 40 cases that I had to review that had prosecution memos written by my staff or had been investigated more and returned. It took me all day! I even worked through lunch. I had the guys bring me a burger and fries back from the dining facility.

Well, I do have a new habit! I started dipping Skoal. I actually started right after Thanksgiving. Tech and Bascombe dip and so does Lt. Faulkner. Tech says he doesn't do it at home though. I am sure I won't do it after I leave this place. Since there is no alcohol, it is the one thing I can do to relax and actually get a buzz. It's a nice escape. I hadn't dipped since I was in junior high. It is such a redneck thing to do; I can't believe I'm doing it. I'm sure once I can have a cold beer after work, I won't do it again. They all get tickled at me when I do it because they say they can hear my country accent even more.

We are playing some games for Christmas. We all drew names, including the guys in the Magistrate Cell. You have to give the person whose name you drew at least three clues about yourself to see if they can guess it is you. I drew Tech's name and I left one clue for him and then one on my day off yesterday. When Tech was at the gym, I called MSgt. Brown on the radio and had him take the two clues I had left in my desk and put them on the wall behind Tech's chair. That way, Tech won't think it's me because he knew I was off and at the hooch. MSgt. Brown isn't playing so he passes out the clues. I have picked clues to make it look like someone else. For example, I said I had a male relation who was a state politician, so he would think it was Lt. Faulkner because I believe his dad held an office. Then I said I played nose guard in football, which I did . . . in 6th grade. He would think I was too small to play that position. Then, I said something about dating women so he would think it was Staff Sergeant Bascombe because he is always talking about women. I have some more that will be good like, I was raised by a nanny my first eight years of life. Lt. Larsen's dad is an Ob/Gyn so he would think it could be him because his family is wealthy.

Oh, I had an opportunity to write down some of the funny sayings LN1 Brown-McDuffie says. She is the Navy paralegal in our office. She talks all the time just like my sister, Stephanie. She always has sayings like… "That's a bunch of butt crack," "with the quickness," "from the rooter to the tooter," "Gots to be more careful," "that's low budget" or "he's low budget," and "he's a nasty rascal." She has us cracking up. It was funny when she told her husband how one of the enlisted guys raised his leg up and farted in the middle of the office. She said she could hear people passing gas at night in their hooch because the plywood that divides the rooms is thin. She can also hear people peeing in the bottles at night. She talks about how Lt. Larsen pees in the bottle at 6:30 pm and still won't go downstairs to use the bathroom! None of the guys blame him because it has gotten really cold.

HOLLYWOOD MEETS REALITY

December 19, 2004, Sunday

Well, the electricity went off about 20 minutes ago, so the only heater we have is off and it's cold outside. I'm writing with a lantern I bought earlier. Today was the USO tour. Karri Turner, the blonde girl on the TV show *JAG* was here. I walked up to her and asked if she would like to meet a real JAG. She smiled and asked, "Are you a real JAG?" I said yes. I told her there were a few of us there and I called my office over. We had a group picture taken.

Then, a wrestler named Bradshaw spoke to the crowd. He has been the longest reigning champion of WWF....I think he said. Mark Wills sang his songs "1980 Something," "Jacob's Ladder," and "The Crowd Goes Wild." He was funny. He wore a USO do-rag on his head and hadn't shaved. He talked about how he appreciated us being there. Then Darryl Worley sang, "What a Beautiful Life," "I Miss My Friend," and "Have You Forgotten." He was real friendly. Also, Al Franken who played Stuart Smalley on *Saturday Night Live* told some jokes. He is now a liberal author and Emmy Award winner. [He became a U.S. Senator in 2008 but resigned in January 2018 after several allegations of sexual misconduct were made against him]. He was funny. He told us how he was at a party in Hollywood and Sylvester Stallone asked him about his USO trips and if he ever felt scared. Al said he did when he flew in a chopper to Tikrit but that was it. Sylvester said "Yeah, that's what I'm talking about....I'm scared something may happen. I've got a good life." Al looked at him and said, "You're freaking Rambo! Rambo shot down a chopper with a bow and arrow!" I'm sure it was all B.S., but it was funny. They put on a good show. They walked around the crowd and just talked to us.

They were there for two hours. They rode a Rhino bus from BIAP to Abu. They have been doing the USO circuit for the past three years. Just down to earth people with no air about them and just very thankful for the troops and proud of the U.S. There were only about 100–150 troops there. Of course, the show was on a stage outside by the dining facility, so we had to wear our body armor and helmets because it was outside. The performers wore their body armor, too. It is hard to get people to come to Abu. BIAP had Robin Williams and John Elway. There was a rumor at BIAP that Abu was getting Christina Aguilera.

CALLING HOME FOR CHRISTMAS

I used a calling card to call the family tonight at 7 pm. It was 10 am in Arkansas. They were all at Stacy and Tim's, my sister and brother-in-law's house. I got to talk to my sister Stacy Lynn, my wife, kids, mom, dad, and my niece and nephew. My son was the first one who wanted to talk to me. He was telling me about how my sister's dog "Bo" loves him and always pulls on him. My daughter wanted to talk to me twice. She wanted her picture taken while she was talking to me. It made me feel good that talking to me meant something to her. She is really looking like a teenager. I know she is, but she is really growing up. Teenagers can be moody, so you have to cherish the memory of any time they show interest in what you're doing as a parent. She won't understand how happy it made me unless she has a teenager someday. They sounded like they were having fun. I'm glad. There is a moment after hanging up the phone and still smiling when your mind becomes conscious again of your physical surroundings. In one moment, you are transported mentally to being with your family, talking, laughing and being part of their Christmas celebration. Then, the next moment you realize you are all alone 6,915 miles away. It is such a joy talking to your family, but you pay the price mentally when the call is over and the stark reality sets in once again. The juxtaposition of the two worlds can really do a number on you. Oh, you want to bask in their comfort, but you don't dare get too comfortable talking to your family. You can't tell them that you are scared, worried, or had a close call because that is unfair to them. Little did I know then that it would be one of the last times I spoke to one of my family members.

Colonel Phelps said he would get us a heater before Christmas. However, we were told that when the General left to go back home, he spent our money on food baskets for people as parting gifts! So, we still have no heaters. Now, we still don't know if the base exchange store at Camp Victory has any heaters to buy even if we do get money. It's been getting colder. There isn't much difference between the living conditions of the detainees and us. We each have winter jackets, hats, and blankets to keep us warm. We have cots and/or a thin mattress to sleep on and we are protected from the wind by a tent or crude hard shelter. I walked around the detainee camps with the Colonel today looking around with MG Brandenburg, the General who replaced General Miller. Only a chain-link fence separating all those detainees from us. The officers in charge of the detainees show they care about the well-being of the detainees. Each week, senior ranking officers visit the detainees, answer their questions, and reassure them their cases are being processed as quickly as possible. If a detainee has a specific question about their case, the General directs us to find the answer and report back. There is one detainee who claims he is from Chicago and was in Iraq visiting his family when he was in the wrong place at the wrong time. I guess prisoners in every country can tell a good story.

ONE STRANGE MOOD

December 22, 2004. Wednesday

    I took off work today. We weren't going to get any files in today but we're getting some Thursday, so I thought I would catch a break. I've read over 3,000 files since I got here in October. I got up about 9 am and watched the movie *Anchor Man* and part of *Cold Mountain*. Then read some. I went and called my wife and talked to my daughter. Superman (my son's nickname) was still asleep. I'm in a funny mood today. Maybe because I coordinated my flight home. Too soon to lose focus here, though. I'm flying out Feb 7th to Kuwait and leaving there on Feb 9th and then to Aviano, Italy, Frankfurt, Germany, and landing in Baltimore, MD by 3 pm on Feb 9th. I have just a little over six weeks. Again, can't let that distract me. Too hard to think about life back home while I'm trying to stay alive over here.

    The mortars started back last night. One hit about 6:30 pm while I was reading in the day room. Needless to say, it shook the dust off the walls that I was sitting beside. Then, about 9 pm another one hit. Again, it rattled the wall by my bed. The sirens didn't go off. So, they must have hit outside the wall. You can just imagine the percussion it would have had if it had landed inside. I can't figure out my mood. It's just feeling less, almost somber. Just strange. Got to stay upbeat for the folks in my office, especially during Christmas. Perhaps my strange mood could be the effects of being mentally alert at all times. Always watching people. Not just while outside the prison but inside the perimeter. We have people from Iraq working at Abu Ghraib, so you don't know who you can trust or who may try to harm you. An Iraqi civilian who works in the laundry drop off location gave me some homemade candy one day. I accepted it with a smile, so as not to offend him, but I didn't eat it. I wasn't willing to take the chance that it hadn't been tampered with. When you are walking outside, you have to scan the area to know where to run in the event a mortar lands or gunfire rings out. In the back of your mind, you know when you walk outside there may not be time to run because your number is up. It's the mortar you don't hear that gets you. One minute you are walking across the field to the office and the next minute you're dead. My mood could also be sadness of being away from my wife and children during Christmas.

SANTA'S COMING

December 23, 2004. Thursday

Well, it was a slow day today. We only got in 75 files, which didn't take too long to review. It was pretty boring. Now, back at the hooch, the lights are out. Luckily, I have a lantern I bought a few weeks ago. It is pitch black in our hooch and I think the generators can't handle all of the use. There are a couple of dryers downstairs (outside). They drain a lot of electricity. They are supposed to stop using them. We don't even have a heater on. Tomorrow is Christmas Eve; it doesn't really feel like it, though. It was pretty warm today, probably low 70s. I am saving the seven presents I have under my tree until Christmas Day. Colonel Phelps is supposed to come in tomorrow at noon. I told everyone they could have half a day off tomorrow. I don't know if his arrival will change those plans. Of course, I told everyone we will be closed all day on Christmas. We are going to have our party at 6 pm on Christmas Eve in the dayroom at our hooch. I hope it goes well. There is a church service tomorrow at 8 pm. So, I figured we would eat at about 5 pm and do the party at 6 pm and then church at 8 pm. I hope the lights are on by then!

Santa came during this week. It was funny seeing him walking around Abu with his Santa suit on and a bulletproof vest over it. You've never seen grown men so happy to see Santa. It wasn't "Santa's Coming!" outbursts like in the move *Elf,* but it was exciting. I guess because it's like a sense of normalcy to see Santa during Christmas. And, yes, he visited offices and passed out candy.

December 27, 2004. Monday

Well, Christmas and Christmas Eve were pretty good.

Lt. Faulkner and I came back to the hooch and decorated for the Christmas Eve party. I hung my lights up and used my Christmas blanket as a tablecloth to put his tree on. We dusted and swept the floors. We chased down near beer, power drinks, and some Mountain Dew for refreshments. We also put out Hickory Farms summer sausage, cheese, and crackers that people in our office had received in care packages. It was mostly eaten.

We didn't have much in the way of gifts to give away to each other for the game. We had to go to the little store and buy things like bicycle reflectors, pink house shoes, etc. One of the Iraqi translators won the pink house shoes. He thought it was funny. After the party, people stuck around and watched the movie *Elf*. I only watched a few minutes of it because I was tired from the day. We closed the office at noon.

We were invited to the Joint Debriefing and Interrogation Center (JDIC) cookout Christmas Eve. They are the guys who "interview" the detainees. We cooked steaks on the grill at about 6 pm and drank "near beer." Then, we headed back to our living area and started our office party at about 7 pm. We played the guessing game to see if we could guess who had given each of us clues. Technical Sergeant Thomas (Tech) didn't guess it was me! I also didn't guess my person. Then we smoked Cuban cigars and started our "dirty" Santa game. For those not familiar with the dirty Santa game, it also goes by less colorful names such as the white elephant game.

All the wrapped presents are placed in a pile. Each person draws a number. The person who drew #1 goes first. They pick any present on the pile and unwrap it. The person with #2 can either take the present from #1 or take a present from the pile and unwrap it. The person with #3 can take the present from #1 or #2 or from the pile and unwrap it. This is repeated until everyone has had a chance to take a present from the pile. When you take a present from another player it is called "stealing" and each gift can only be stolen three times. If you select an unpopular present from the pile, then there is a good chance no one will steal it and you will be taking it home. As I mentioned earlier, the unwrapped present the Iraqi translator selected was a pair of pink house shoes. That is why he left with them at the end of the night.

Colonel Phelps said we had to keep the office open Christmas Day. I wasn't going to make anyone work Christmas Day, so I worked it alone. I went in at 8 am and worked until about 6 pm, then I watched *Seinfeld* episodes and surfed the internet. I called home and spoke to my wife and my parents. The kids were already lying down for the night. I called back at 6 pm my time and talked to the kids about what they had gotten for Christmas. They both seemed happy. I came home to my room and opened up the gifts my mom had sent me. I got several books, which I needed. I have about 39 days left. It has started to get old around here. It has a way of wearing you down.

A LITTLE SURGERY

December 28, 2004. Tuesday

Got up this morning and waited in line to cash a check. Finance only comes once every two weeks. I got there an hour early, so I was fourth in line. The line for postal service was about two hours, I didn't have anything to mail. I got to the office about 8:30 am and went to sick call to see about my fourth toe on my left foot. I had this bump about the size of my pinky toenail growing on the side near my third toe. It came up overnight and has been there for over a month. I thought it was a callous or a corn because my socks were tight. I found out it was a wart! They gave me three shots in my toe to numb it. It hurt like heck. I could feel them pushing the needle further and further into my toe. Luckily, the doctor had a 27-gauge needle in his hooch that he ran and got. Otherwise, it would have been a 10-gauge, which was huge. After the shots, my toe bled because the doctor had hit a vein. Then, he cut the wart off and cauterized it to stop the bleeding. The cauterizer went out so he couldn't finish it. So, he said it would bleed through the bandage. I can't wear my boots today, but I can take the bandage off tomorrow, use a band-aid, and then wear my boot. I told him I didn't want to have to wear a tennis shoe or medical boot with my uniform. I always hated seeing people wearing tennis shoes in uniform. So, I hobbled back to the office with just my sock. He gave me Motrin and Tylenol 3 for the pain.

I had the guys bring me lunch back, and I'm cooking an MRE in my room for supper. I will take tomorrow off anyway. I reviewed 90 files today, but Lt. Larsen did some too.

At the force protection meeting, we learned that there will probably be an attack on January 1st, and it may involve the prisoners at the hard site, which houses violators of local laws. On Christmas Eve, two cars drove up to the entry control point at the front gate of Abu and didn't stop. The tower shot them. The cars stopped, turned around, and drove away. I guess we didn't kill all of them. Well, my MRE should be hot by now. I guess I will eat it and listen to Nickelback on the CD player.

December 29, 2004. Wednesday

Well, today was a day of much-needed rest. I woke up about 8:30 am and remembered I had a meeting at 9 am or 9:30 am, so I called the office on the radio. "JAG 2 this is JAG 1, over." Lt. Faulkner answered and I told him about the meeting I needed him to cover for me. He said my wife called and was calling back in 20 minutes and that she knew I had a radio and that she wanted the office to call me and have me come in. He told her 20 minutes was too quick, assuming he could reach me on the radio. They settled on 30. MSgt. Brown told me that everyone disappeared from the office because they didn't want to take the call when she called back. They said they knew they were going to be in trouble with my wife if I didn't come in and would be in trouble by me if they woke me up or didn't tell me she called and was calling back. So, when I had Lt. Faulkner on the radio telling him about the meeting, I told him to tell her that I had surgery on my toe, and I wasn't coming in today. MSgt. Brown took the call when she called back. He said she got all spun up when they told her "I got cut on" and was laid up. They all love telling me about her demeanor when she calls. Everyone asked me today if I called her back. I can barely walk, there is no way I am putting on a boot today.

When I got up this morning, I tried removing the tape that was wrapped all around my foot and ankle. I pulled many hairs out of my foot and leg. I then tried to remove the bandage, but it was stuck to the cut because of all the dried blood. There was enough blood to cover two 50-cent pieces. I had to wet the bandage to get it to come loose. The cut was open and not scabbed. So, I left the bandage off for the day. I had to take a Tylenol 3 before I could even pull the bandage off because of the pain. Of course, Tylenol 3 made me sleepy, so I went back to bed. I woke up at 4 pm. Now, I have a nice scab on the toe. The cut itself is about half the size of a dime. I got in the shower and now letting it scab some more before putting a band-aid on it. I didn't eat breakfast or lunch. I had a package of crackers. I need to find something to eat. My room needed cleaning today, but it will have to wait. We finally received a couple of more small space heaters for our living quarters. There are only a few things here that make this place tolerable, such as all you can eat free food and good people. When the temperature drops, a heater is quickly added to that list.

POST HOLIDAY BLUES

December 31, 2004. Friday

    As I sat on the edge of my cot with the orange glow from the heater echoing off the wooden walls, the clock showed midnight. New Year! The time, the minute, the hour was as fleeting as the previous ones. The quiet wasn't disturbed. Only one person stirring and walking to the restroom. I sit in silence reading a mystery novel I had received for Christmas. What a strange time, sitting in an Iraqi prison with a lack of celebration for what a new year will bring us. As I pen these few lines, eager to go to sleep, I look forward to having a year full of happiness. As I reflect on my life and future, I can honestly say that God has been the constant; the one thing that I could depend on.

    It is during these quiet moments, which I don't have enough of due to a hectic schedule, I can reflect on life. I know I didn't accomplish my goals by myself. I like to think I am slightly above average on the smart scale, but I know I wouldn't have made it without God giving me some breaks. I know I am not going to stay alive over here solely by my own wits. I have been a Christian since I was 10 years old, but admittedly, I didn't fully appreciate the power of prayer until I had struggles. Before I deployed, my Aunt Joyce and Uncle Jerry, who were missionaries in Africa for many years, told me that they added my name to their prayer list. They had a group of friends who would pray for specific people going through specific troubles. I didn't think much about it at the time, but during these quiet times, I feel that I have been protected. It is easy to say you don't need God when things are going well, but perhaps things are going well because you needed and turned to God. I had always heard that there are no atheists in foxholes, but I know that isn't true because one of the guys in my office claims to be an atheist. Nevertheless, when you are in a dangerous situation, such as being constantly mortared, you realize that death is a real possibility, and you think about what you've done with your life. Did I waste the chances I have been given?

You don't need to be a Christian to be a good person, and I hope that being a Christian is not the *only* reason I try to be a good person. It may sound odd that a Christian is prosecuting or deciding the fate of a Muslim, but religion plays no role in what I do here. There are other principles at play. The principles of fairness and due process aren't only part of my personal life, but part of my professional life. I view my role here as a referee. A person is suspected of harming or attempting to harm a member of the coalition forces. I look to see whether there is evidence to agree with the accuser or the detainee. In the end, it isn't a Christian or American who decides the fate of the detainee. His fellow countryman, Iraqi board members or Iraqi judges, determine whether he is a security threat or guilty of a crime. I can only ensure the part in which I am involved is a fair process. It just so happens that my role coincides with my personal and professional beliefs.

I have given everyone the morning off tomorrow. However, I must go in at 8 am to get it all going. It's going to be the first time in a long time that New Year's came and went without any celebration on my part. It's different now. I have a different outlook on life and want to start enjoying life differently. This is a good place to start.

Over the years, I viewed New Year's as a party. Drinking too much, staying up too late, sleeping in the next day. I didn't use it as an opportunity to reflect on things that happened over the last year, what I liked and didn't like about what I had done, or what I planned to change in the coming year. Sitting in a combat zone, you realize that you may not get another chance to improve your life, to become a better husband, father, or son. You think about the time you have wasted and how it could have been spent. I have always been goal-driven. Go to college, get married, have children, become a lawyer, get selected into the Air Force JAG Corps. I didn't slow down to reflect. Then, as a father, I started pushing my children to accomplish goals that I believed were important. I can say my perspective has changed over the last couple of months. What is important has changed. Yes, I still want my kids to grow up and be successful, but the question now is successful at what? I don't mean which career. I mean I want them to be good people, fair people, caring people, and honest people. I now see my priority as a parent as helping my kids get into Heaven and not Harvard. Of course, Harvard would be nice, too, if it came with a scholarship!

WAR TROPHIES

January 1, 2005. Saturday

I came in and worked from 8 am until 2 pm. I let everyone come in at noon. I woke up with a terrible sinus head. Just my luck. Even when I don't drink a drop of alcohol during the New Year's Eve celebration, I still wake up with a headache.

January 5, 2005. Wednesday

Today was my day off; however, I came in to receive my wife's phone call. It has been almost a week since the guys told her I had "been cut on." They made it sound like major surgery! We have gotten into a routine in which she calls on Wednesday if I don't call her. It gives me some comfort knowing I will get to hear her voice once a week. I can't tell her about my travel plans to get home because it's a security risk. All military members know you don't discuss travel on an unsecured line because you don't know who could be listening. If the bad guys know when and where you are traveling, then they have time to coordinate an attack. It isn't the words that are important, though. She can tell by my voice that I am excited about preparing for my trip home. I can hear the giddiness in her voice. We are like two young lovers despite having been together for 20 years. A military member does not serve and sacrifice alone. The whole family sacrifices. Birthdays and holiday are missed with each other, having to move often, and leaving friends behind, and the spouse, of course, is at home keeping it all together.

I also had to finish reviewing the files I didn't finish yesterday. I then went to the property room and picked out some items they were getting rid of. The property room is a large room where the things taken off prisoners are stored. Some of the items couldn't be connected to a case and some couldn't be connected to an owner. I selected a bayonet for an AK 47, two small pocket knives, a short sword in a silver sheath, a scope for some type of a rifle, and an Iraq license plate. I still have to fill out the war souvenir forms and get it signed by a lieutenant colonel or higher, so I can take them home. I definitely don't want to get in trouble for taking souvenirs without proper authorization. It shouldn't be a problem because the items meet the criteria of what is authorized in the "Frago" signed by Lt. Gen Sanchez.

RECORD OF ATTACKS

I learned some interesting stuff today about the attacks on Abu Ghraib. Between September and December 2004, there have been 121 mortars that have landed on the base and exploded. Many others didn't explode. The breakdown is like this. September had 47 rounds in five attacks; October was 17 rounds in six attacks; November was 55 rounds in 13 attacks and December was two rounds in one attack. Many times we hear the explosion outside the base and it shakes our buildings. We had at least one a day for the last four days. Today, one shook the front door of the building where we work. It must have landed outside the base because they didn't sound the siren.

I ended up working all day today. Just when I finished all the files from the day before, they brought me a full box of about 100 or so more. I did watch *Scorpion King* on my computer at work with headphones. I may try to get out of the office early tomorrow if I finish reviewing the files.

I just found out today that our trip to the Marine Expeditionary Force (MEF) to train them on collecting evidence is back on. I think they are in Ramadi. They don't want us to come because they have their own attorneys and don't think they need our help. However, they send us very bad files with witness statements that are unclear and have no pictures of weapons, which the Iraqi judges want to see at trial. Their statistics on how many of their cases can be prosecuted are bad and I reported it to their colonel. I never heard back from them.

I have read about 3,500 files since I have arrived in Abu on Oct 11th. That's over 1,000 a month. The attorneys in my office only review the ones I mark as "prosecute" or "more investigation." Those are only about 25% of the cases. I believe the conviction rate at the court is still about 75%.

THE TORTURE TOUR

I toured the death house again at Abu when some new guys from Camp Victory came down for the day to pick up the case files and bring us supplies. The death house is what we call the building that has the gallows inside. It's where Saddam and his sons would hang people. There are a few holding cells, just like jail cells, next to the room where the gallows stand. The people in the cells could undoubtedly hear the trap doors of the gallows swing open as they awaited their turn. Of course, they may have been lined up against the wall outside which was also used as a method of execution. I photographed the bloody handprint on the inside of the holding cell wall in the death house. I imagine the people were beaten before being dragged to the gallows. It was pretty freaky. Especially the little room underneath the hanging platform where they burned clothing, shoes, other personal property, and maybe the people, too. There are still old shoes and stuff in there.

MSgt. Brown went to Bucca this week to scout out resources and to look at the new office space. He has a background in supply and seemed like the logical choice to go. He went with some other folks from Camp Victory. He is coming back to Abu tomorrow morning.

January 6, 2005. Thursday

Today was a heck of a day. I pulled up stats and found out that I have received 3,769 cases since October 11. Only 639 cases were referred for prosecution…17%.

KINKS IN THE CHAIN

I had a tense email discussion with Lt. Colonel McLaughlin at the embassy because he visited the Marine Expeditionary Force (MEF) to train them on collecting evidence. It seems that the embassy legal office is duplicating my office's work. I don't understand why it is necessary for me to send my guys to Ramadi to train soldiers if the attorneys at the embassy are going out there, too. It upsets me on both a professional and personal level. On a professional level, my staff is wasting hours assembling evidence, researching Iraqi laws, and writing memos that the embassy legal office seems to not be reading. On a personal level, I am sending attorneys and paralegals on trips throughout Iraq to train soldiers on collecting evidence when it is already being done by the attorneys at the embassy. Anytime a person leaves the perimeter of Abu, their risk of death increases. We all understand the risk when it is for the mission, but when you risk a person's life by sending them on a mission that was unnecessary, you have to be held accountable. You have to be accountable not only on a professional level, but on a personal level. You have to live with the fact that you unnecessarily put a person in harm's way and they were killed.

I proposed in an email to Colonel Phelps and Lt. Colonel McLaughlin that we should reorganize by leaving an officer in charge at Abu, me, to review files, and a law office manager to manage the case database and a couple of paralegals for support. And then assign a much-needed additional attorney to the Magistrate Cell to assist with determining whether there is probable cause to detain a prisoner. The rest of the staff could be transferred to the embassy legal office where they would be responsible for training troops, collecting evidence, and preparing cases for prosecution. I figured I'd get a call from Colonel Phelps and get my butt chewed after he read the email but I didn't

I called home to talk to the kids but they were asleep and I didn't want to talk long. I think I was grumpy to my wife. I'm usually pretty good at compartmentalizing my work problems from my personal life, but this time the frustration I had with the organizational structure here was too much. It was icing over at home in Southwest Oklahoma, and the kids weren't going to go to school until later in the day. I don't like it when the kids miss school, especially since they missed school before Christmas break to go visit my family in Arkansas. Also, my car back home hasn't been driven in two weeks. It is probably good that I didn't talk long because I only have a certain amount of space to put my frustration. I guess my frustration about work left no room for the frustration I had about my personal life.

I am tired and ready to go home and just relax. I am tired of people trying to kill me and it makes matters worse when the officers I work with are fighting with each other. The work isn't hard, just frustrating. I have about 29 days to go before I leave Abu on Feb 5th to fly out of BIAP on Feb 7th.

Tomorrow, I need to work on a continuity binder to help out the people who are replacing me. I had no guidance on what to do or how to do it when I arrived, so I will try to make it easier for the next group of people who replace me. I am the 3rd team of JSLET/TF 134 Detention Ops, but the first one to operate out of Abu. A lot of rules and procedures change as the detainee process is improved.

I went to the port-a-potty a minute ago and heard the perimeter towers firing at people. I don't even flinch anymore. There are many superstitions in combat, and one is most people get killed their last month in a combat zone because they become complacent. So, I have to remember that. When I first arrived here, I had already made peace with God and had accepted the fact that I may get killed. Now that I am in my last month here and can see the light at the end of the tunnel, I want to live! I'm tired and need to pick an MRE (meal ready to eat—meal not fit to eat is more like it) for supper.

January 7, 2005. Friday

Well, I'm still fighting with the embassy legal office. Colonel Phelps is mad about it and told us to meet him at the embassy to talk on Jan 12th. The International Committee of the Red Cross came to my office today. I spoke with an attorney from Switzerland who is part of the Committee. He isn't the legal adviser, just a member. He had questions about our office function and the Iraqi court. It went pretty well. He seemed pleased and impressed that I have a 24-hour turn around on the cases I receive. We work hard here to ensure the detainees have speedy due process.

PRISONER ESCAPE

January 10, 2005. Monday

This morning wasn't as exciting as yesterday morning. Yesterday, we were woken up about 6:30 am to a siren. I yelled "Get it on!" and we all put on our armored vests and Kevlar helmets, grabbed our weapons, and took our fighting positions that I had previously set up in our living quarters when I first arrived.

We learned that a prisoner in Level 5 (the highest) had escaped. He was in solitary confinement surrounded by four walls of cyclone fence in an area shaped like a horseshoe. The door was made of an old bed frame that had a passthrough at the bottom to give him food and to cuff him prior to letting him out. He pulled the door open enough to slip through. Then, he traveled halfway across Abu along the brick wall and then climbed the wall by Tower 2. He then had to climb a cyclone fence with razor wire. We found his socks that he had used to grab the razor wire. He is gone! It happens periodically. It was still dark when he escaped, and it wasn't discovered until shift change at 6:30 am.

Well, I am headed to work this morning. Dragging a little because I was up until midnight reading a book. I tend to read books about attorneys or detectives because those are the things that I'm most familiar with and can relate to. I work with both back home and here in the desert. I also like books written by attorneys. I've read all of the books written by John Grisham, who was an attorney in Mississippi before becoming an author.

January 11, 2005. Tuesday

Let's see. I forgot to mention that yesterday I saw a Humvee pull up to the hospital door, which is about 30 feet from our office door, and take in a U.S. Army gunner. These are the guys who ride with their upper body above the roof of the truck so they can operate a mounted weapon. An IED blast had hit the truck, but only the gunner was injured; he took shrapnel to the neck. I saw soldiers standing around the truck cleaning the blood out of the truck. People who saw them take the gunner inside said people were covered in blood. They medevac'd him out a few minutes later. The hospital here is used to treat the detainees. Many of the detainees in the hospital were injured during their capture, usually from a fire fight or after an IED. When I go inside the hospital for meetings, I have to sign my weapon into a secured storage room, so no one has a weapon inside the hospital. I guess that removes the chances of a detainee grabbing someone's weapon and shooting the place up.

GETTING CLOSER

Today, we had a couple of mortars go off right as we were walking out of the office to go to lunch. We later learned it had landed 200 meters outside the base. Amazingly, it can rattle our doors and shake our building from that far away.

I'm going to watch the military polygraph examiner administer a polygraph to a detainee tomorrow. I happened to meet an Air Force Office of Special Investigation (OSI) agent named Taylor. I can't remember his first name. I asked him if I could watch a polygraph exam or interrogation of a detainee and he said sure. His partner called me today and said they have one scheduled for 8 am tomorrow.

Last night, a guy who lives on the first floor of our living quarters came to our area and said I needed to go to my office. I found out that Colonel Phelps called the Magistrate Cell looking for us at 8:30 pm. He wanted us to scan two files. Then, I had to walk to the JDIC, which is the joint interrogation office, to see if they had one of the files that Colonel Phelps wanted. I knew they didn't because, according to our case data system, I had already forwarded it to Camp Victory. But, to please Colonel Phelps, I walked to JDIC and checked. I got back to my room at about 9:30 pm. I told guys working in the Magistrate Cell to not answer the phone at night anymore when they're there goofing off. Colonel Phelps had tracked me down by calling the Magistrate Cell who contacted someone they knew in their living area, who tracked me down. That is the second night in a row I have been chased down after being settled in my room after a long day. The first night, Master Sergeant Brown had to go to the office after hours to get files. The Magistrate Cell attorneys work late because they only have 48 hours to review a detainee's file starting when the detainee first arrives. If the Magistrate Cell determines there is probable cause to believe the detainee is a security threat or violated Iraqi laws, then they forward the case to my office to determine whether it should be prosecuted or sent to the board. The JDIC will also review files if the detainee has potential information for intelligence purposes. Well, I guess I'll finish reading my book, *Cinderella Affidavit*, and go to bed.

WATCHING DETAINEE INTERROGATIONS

January 12, 2005. Wednesday

I went to watch a polygraph of a detainee this morning. But due to some scheduling issues, the interrogator wasn't there. I went back at 1 pm. They interrogated/polygraphed a guy caught last night. They had a picture of him holding a rifle with an explosion behind him. It was an attack on a convoy near Abu. There were pictures of dead American civilians and people holding up boots of a civilian. The detainee today was deceptive on test questions when he denied ever participating in attacks on coalition forces.

The interrogation room is a room of plywood inside a Conex storage container (like a railway car). I was in the next room watching it on a monitor and wearing headphones. I watched it with an interrogator and an analyst. The detainee was in the next room with the polygrapher and interpreter. The interpreter sat behind the detainee. It was a real neat experience. It lasted for about two and a half hours. They videotaped the whole thing, so the detainee doesn't accuse us of mistreating him.

CRACKS IN THE OFFICE

January 13, 2005. Thursday

I found out today that my meeting with Colonel Phelps and Lt. Colonel McLaughlin at the embassy legal office on Saturday is canceled. We may try to meet Monday. We requested a helicopter, but we won't know until the day before if we will get one. I asked Colonel Phelps if he minded if Lt. Larsen goes along so he can see a trial at CCCI. He said that would be fine. Anytime you send someone out, you need to be able to justify it as important in case things go bad.

LN1 our Navy paralegal leaves Abu tomorrow to work at Camp Victory for a week, then she flies home to San Diego. She has been away from home for six months. I have 23 days until Feb 5th when I go to BIAP and leave BIAP on Feb 7th. I went and got a haircut today. I have been going on Fridays, not because I need a haircut but because I needed the massage. I go once a week regardless if I need a haircut. The haircut is $3 and I tip one or two dollars depending on how long the massage aka head thumbing lasts. They call it "shocking the brain." The Indians do it. They slap your forehead, massage your eyebrows, slap the back of your neck, and massage your scalp. Then they put their hands together and hit you in the head and make this popping noise. It reminded me of the sound we would make as kids by opening our mouths and tapping our knuckles on our skull. Another way to describe it is like knocking on a hollow tree trunk. It's wild! Maybe it was their inside joke to make it sound like our heads were hollow.

I'm putting together a continuity binder for our replacements. I have also started writing letters to my staff members' bosses back home to tell them of the good work they are doing here. Everyone is tired and wants to go home. I've had to do a lot of mentoring and really learned to become a leader in a combat zone. One of the best compliments I received from Colonel Phelps is how I was able to keep my staff motivated and in good spirits despite their poor living and working conditions and being under constant mortar attacks. I often think of my style of leadership being a participative leadership style. I involve staff members in the decision process by seeking their input. I find it motivates the team because they have a personal interest in the plan. It often leads to creativity and productivity. Don't misunderstand. I have no issue with making decisions. I had to revert to an authoritarian leadership style at times when I found the team was engaging in too much talk and not enough action or the collaboration had been replaced with arguments and resistance. However, I have worked for people who have an authoritarian leadership style and I speak from experience when I say it shouldn't be used often due to the collapse of synergy and collaboration. It can gut an organization quickly.

I've seen staff turn on a general officer who used the authoritarian leadership style and it cost the general his job. It is easy in the military to use the authoritarian leadership style. We call it "pulling rank." I outrank you so you do what I say, no questions asked. That is equivalent to a parent telling the child to do it because I told you so. It teaches nothing and is shortsighted. There is a time when each style is appropriate, and it depends partly on the personalities of your team and urgency of the situation. As I told the team when I first arrived, let's have fun, be safe, and accomplish the mission. There is a time and place for humor in the business setting and in the military setting. Good leaders know when to use the right leadership style and humor at the right time. If you want a good discussion on leadership, just ask your boss if they want people to follow him because they love him or fear him.

I had our Army Specialist come into the office crying a couple of days ago. He thought everyone was giving him the worst jobs and assignments. I called him into my office to ask him what was going on. He was still crying. I told him about how he will get the least favorite taskings often because he is the lowest ranking person in the office. I also pointed out that everyone in the office is pitching in. We have a technical sergeant taking out the trash, staff sergeant looking for files, and a lieutenant clearing out the supply room. I talked to him about stepping up and doing things that he sees need to be done instead of waiting to be told.

He was reading a magazine and Lt. Larsen was reviewing files, so I asked the Specialist to punch holes in the paper in the files and fasten them in the folder. The Specialist said he couldn't because he had other work to do. I replied to that with, "You better not have any other work to do if you're in there reading a magazine." I asked him who he thought should punch holes and he said the person reviewing the case…. implying me. Then, before I had the chance to lay into him, Technical Sergeant Thomas came out of the supply room. Technical Sergeant Thomas is usually quiet, but he said, "I can't believe we have an E-4 saying the 0-4 Major should be punching holes in papers." I explained to the Specialist why it was inefficient for the reviewer to punch holes in the files. Instead of just using the "rank" as a justification, I gave him the practical reason, too. I explained to him that the reviewer is usually reviewing a stack of 100 files at a time. The reviewer can get into a "zone," and review quickly, and make the decision whether a case should be prosecuted or sent to the CRRB.

I asked the Marine JAG, who is the attorney who works with the Specialist, if he wanted to talk to him or if he wanted me to talk to him. He said I should because he had gotten too close with the Specialist and had become more of a big brother to him instead of his superior officer. It was good for him to recognize that problem. Except for Lt. Wall, the officers in the office have been in the military for about two years and need mentoring. Lt. Wall is being considered for promotion to the rank of lieutenant commander. That is equivalent to a major in the Air Force. When a person is being considered for promotion, we call it "meeting the board" because it is a group of people who review your personnel file. They compare your record to others also meeting the board. The board will decide what percentage of the people will be selected.

Anyway, when I talked to the Specialist later, I also explained to him about learning to become a problem-solver and not acting like a "know-it-all." I told him that he was smart, but a person isn't successful unless they can prove to someone that they are right without making the other person mad. It's about having tact. I told him about selling himself/his personality to people was like selling a car. If you are selling to a mom, you emphasize safety and if it's man, you emphasize how sporty it is. I told him to identify what he was trying to accomplish, find out what would be persuasive to the person he is speaking with, and sell yourself as a go-getter, without being a know-it-all. I told him how I play the dumb country boy, which is my form of deliberate manipulation to lower other people's expectations to give me the advantage in every situation. I think I got through to him. He talked to me several times that day about how to do it. He even had to tell our Air Force airman that the number of files she brought us didn't match the number listed on the paper. He did a good job showing her he was right and did it without making her mad.

I told them that I will identify problems and it is up to them to solve them. That way they can grow. They know the mission and they can figure out the details such as how to schedule trips to different parts of Iraq, developing training aids and PowerPoint presentations, developing contacts, etc.

It has been a learning process for all of us. You can start seeing the tension sometimes. People are missing their family and this place can wear you out by just living and breathing here. And, we work and live together, eat together, and try to stay alive together, and that can be way too much time together.

January 14, 2005. Friday

Today, nothing exciting to report. The motor pool finally came and got our truck. The unit that loaned it to us is moving out of Abu and had to take it. It was very useful over the last three months.

Just riding out the next 22 days. I have taken up a couple of bad habits since I've been here. I started dipping a couple of months ago, and this week, I have been smoking a few cigarettes. Just trying to find something to make this place a little more something, not enjoyable because that is asking too much. Just trying to find something to make this place a little more tolerable. The work isn't what makes it stressful, it's just this place over time. I'm sure I'll drop both habits when I get home.

My flip-flops wore out a couple of nights ago. I had to duct tape around my left flip-flop because the top part started pulling away from the sole. It only has to hold for three weeks. I need them when I take a shower, and anytime I take off my boots.

I decided to take a shower in the building connected to our living quarters. The shower is right inside the door where the guys ran when the mortars landed. For some reason, using this shower tonight seemed like the safer choice than walking across a dirt field to the shower sheds. If a mortar lands near you when you are in the field, then that is pretty much it for you. Unfortunately, tonight the lights were out in the shower. Imagine a hallway with brick stalls and no windows. I propped the door open and took a shower in the dark. Hey, it's my body. I know where all the parts are.

Went to the gym today. I've been going every other day lately. I'm still up to 145 lbs. That's the heaviest I have ever been. Well, I guess I will get an MRE and watch a movie.

CHINESE TAKE-OUT IN BAGHDAD

January 18, 2005. Tuesday

Lt. Larsen and I caught a chopper to the embassy yesterday at about 2 pm. I went to have the meeting with Lt. Colonel McLaughlin and Colonel Phelps. We ordered Chinese food from downtown Baghdad and had it delivered to the embassy gate. Not bad Chinese food for Baghdad.

We didn't finish our meeting until after 10 pm. We met on the first floor of the palace in one of Saddam's fancy conference rooms. It had nice furniture and three mirrored walls. A very formal setting. I brought my can of Skoal and commented to the Colonel that I bet ole Saddam never expected an American to be in here chewing tobacco. It reminded me of the Toby Keith song "Who's That Man?" where he sings "that's my house and that's my car" and then asks, "who's that man, running my life?"

Since the meeting lasted so long, Lt. Larsen and I decided to sleep on cots in the embassy legal office instead of trying to get back to Abu late at night. I had a blanket and was fine. We got a lot accomplished at the meeting. Finally, we are going to restructure the organization and combine the Abu and embassy legal offices to cut down on duplication of work and to make it more efficient. We caught the chopper back to Abu about 11:30 am today. It's about a 20-minute flight, and I took some good pictures. Well, I'm tired and going to crash. I only have about 17 days left at Abu and then head to Camp Victory to out process and go home.

January 20, 2005. Thursday

Last night, I came home and went to bed at about 6:30 pm. I was exhausted. Read about 4500 files since Oct 11th. At 8:30 pm the sirens went off. I had to gear up and man the fighting positions in our living area. A rocket landed by Tower 5. After a few minutes, everything went back to normal.

I slept until 9:30 am this morning. I took a shower, took my clothes to the laundry, and ate lunch. I watched the first two *Lord of the Rings* movies. Those are about three hours apiece. I had seen the second one before the first one and then watched the first one a couple of years ago. So, today, I tried to watch the third one, but I couldn't remember what the first two were about, so I decided to start with the first one. I watched the first two from 12 pm to 6 pm. Then I started the third one. I didn't watch all of it. We all started watching *Conan the Barbarian*. Now, that one I hadn't seen in 20 years. It was pretty good. So, today, on my day off, I sat in a bean bag for nine hours on a dirty concrete floor. I hope I can sleep tonight. It is 9:30 pm. I will read and then try to get sleepy.

We got over 100 files today. Lt. Larsen reviewed some of them for me. He commented that he didn't know how I read all those files. Once you get in a "zone" you can get through them at a decent pace. There are usually less than 10 pages in each file.

I only have about two weeks left at Abu and then I go to BIAP to out process. I'm ready to get back to the real world.

A WAKE-UP CALL

January 21, 2005. Friday

Got to work at 8 am. At about 8:15 am the sirens went off. We put on our gear. Right before the sirens sounded a huge explosion occurred. It was probably the loudest I had heard. We got a call that our living area had been hit! Then another call that a mortar had landed in the room of our Marine JAG, which is right beside mine. He wanted to leave the office to go check on it. Another Captain told him no because it was still too dangerous outside. They got in an argument with one of them blocking the door. I was on the phone with my wife when MSgt. Brown told me that he hated to interrupt but we have a "situation." I hung up the phone. He briefed me and I went up to the Marine JAG and told him he wasn't leaving. He said, "Yes, sir."

About an hour later it was all clear and we went to check out the damage. Sure enough, a mortar had crashed into the ceiling in between my room and the Marine JAG's room. It hadn't fully exploded.

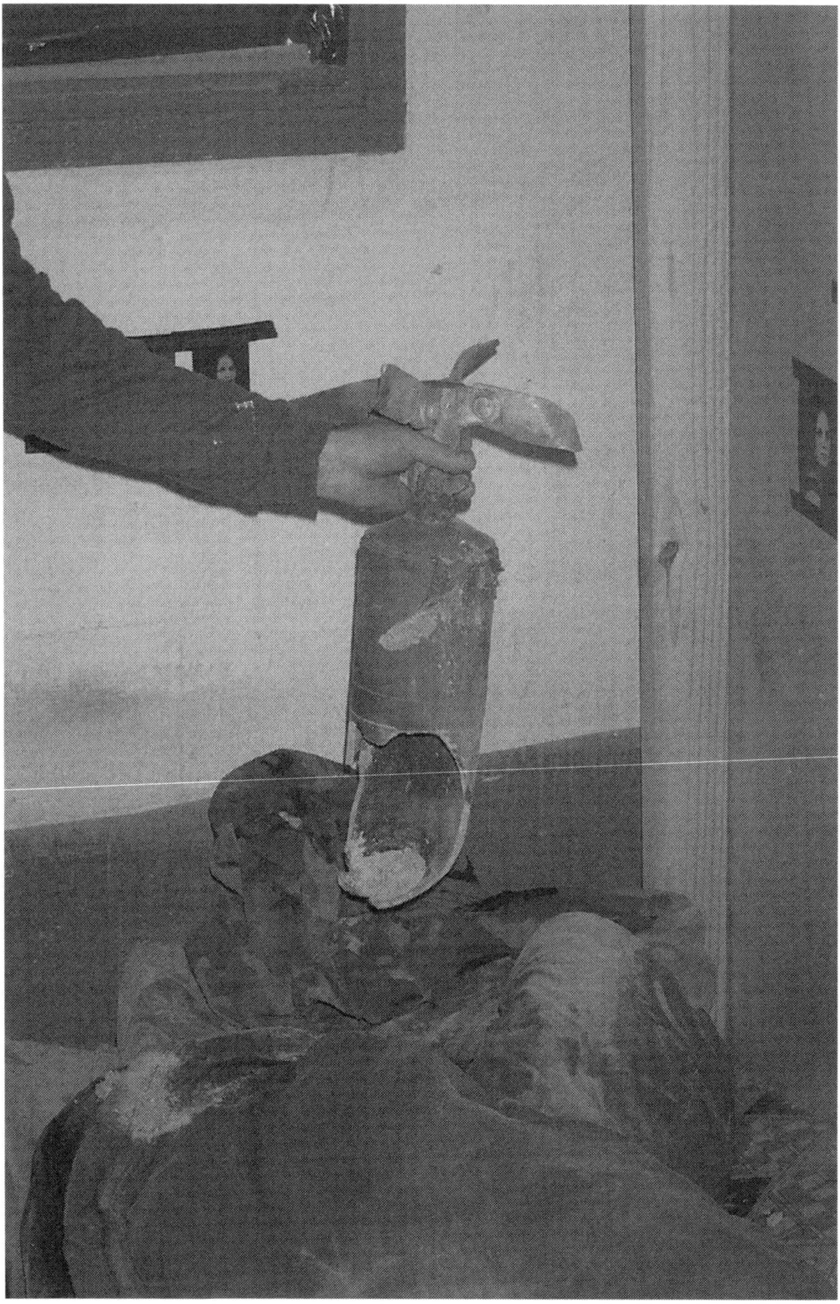

It crashed through the concrete ceiling of our living area turning concrete pieces from the ceiling into projectiles.

It destroyed his computer, his DVD player, and sprayed his room with chunks of concrete and powder. His room is next to mine. It landed about 10 feet from my bed.

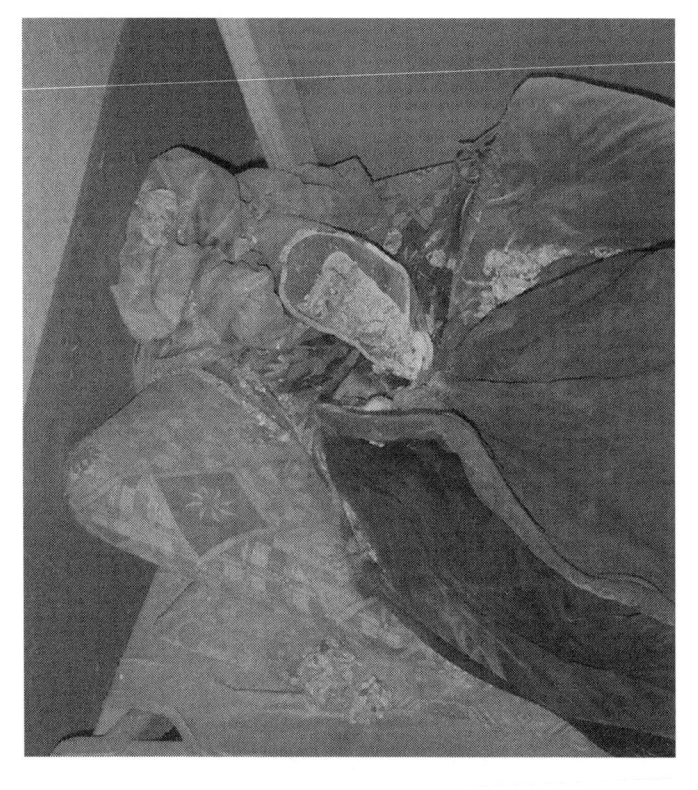

It also crashed into Specialist Campbell's room. In fact, the actual mortar, at least what was left of it, landed on Specialist Campbell's pillow on his cot. He would have been killed if it had been his day off.

Luckily, he was off the day before along with the Marine JAG. I usually take Fridays off, but I've been switching up just depending on the workload. I'm glad I went to work on my day off! The superstition of dying during your last 30 days of deployment almost came true.

We took a lot of pictures of the damage. Many people came in to look. The Marine JAG was pretty shaken up by it. He decided to go to "Combat Stress," the medical office that counsels soldiers who are stressed. We didn't want to leave him alone, so when the Specialist was going to lunch, I came by and stayed with him. Finally, the doctor came by the office and dragged him to lunch. The Specialist is fine with the mortar incident. He and the Marine JAG moved to rooms on the other side of the hall. Their rooms were too destroyed to clean up. We believe tomorrow will be another big day. It is getting closer to the elections on Jan 30th and it is also some special day for Iraq.

Just a little color commentary to explain why the election is such a big deal. It will be the first democratic election in Iraq in more than 30 years. Over 80% of Iraqis polled said they intend to vote for the provincial councils for each of Iraq's provinces. The council will comprise of 275 members and make up the Transitional National Assembly (TNA). The TNA will elect the President and Vice Presidents, who will in turn unanimously select the Prime Minister, who then must be approved by the TNA. Helping the Iraqis create a democracy is one of the primary purposes of us being here. Sure, when Saddam was in power, they held "elections" and strangely he received 100% of the votes. Of course, the jihadists aren't happy about the elections.

The ceiling in our living area is pretty thick, but we now know that if something wants to come through, then it will. The ceiling also had steel rods in the concrete and that still didn't stop the mortar.

The angle it hit showed it was fired from the south or southwest. It is kind of freaky thinking about what would happen if it came through a wall. Especially since I lie against a wall, and that wall faces west where I can see the apartments off base. Everyone is nervous, but no one says anything. This is a good reminder that complacency kills. Sometimes staying alive is a matter of not being in the wrong place at the wrong time. I have two weeks from tomorrow, and anything can still happen at any time.

FIRE FIGHTS AND NEWS REPORTING

January 26, 2005. Wednesday

Not a whole lot going on the last few days, except two firefights about 8:30 pm. Then a loud explosion woke me up at 3 am. I found out Tower 1, the one I worked a couple of months ago, shot at a couple of guys who were carrying AK 47s. The suspects then ran to an area which was in the firing sector of Tower 9, so Tower 9 shot at them. No word on whether we killed them. The explosion was a VBIED (a car with explosives) that was found and exploded.

Peter Jennings, the *ABC News* correspondent, will be at Abu tomorrow. I think he is doing a story on detainee abuse. Go figure. I will see if I can run into him and get a picture. I have had a very bad headache all day. I've taken about 2000 mg of Tylenol today; it is finally starting to go away.

It's still cold and muddy here. Mud is everywhere. I think I may take my day off tomorrow even though it isn't Friday, my usual day off. But I'll miss out on seeing Peter Jennings. It's a good thing I changed it a few weeks ago since last Friday the mortar crashed through the room next to mine.

We have had a Navy JAG here this week. He came to defend a Marine in a special court-martial for testing positive for cocaine and confessing to using drugs. He has been hanging out in our office.

Technical Sergeant Thomas is leaving Friday. He wasn't supposed to leave until Monday, but they are stopping convoys because of the election on Jan 30th and they expect more attacks.

Well, I think I will stretch out for a few minutes. I'm passing on the gym today because of my headache. I have nine days left at Abu if I leave on Feb 5th. I may leave a day early just to make sure I get all my paperwork done in time. Staff Sergeant Shively, my paralegal from back home, is leaving the embassy legal office on Feb 4th.

I finished all the letters of appreciation for everyone in my office.

I also heard that the new general, MG Brandenburg, is downgrading everyone's awards, so I may not get a Bronze Star that Colonel Phelps put me in for.

I wrote an awards package to support MSgt. Brown receiving a Meritorious Service Medal. I sent it up again lobbying for an MSM, but I don't know if they will change it. I tried to grease the wheels, so to speak, when I submitted bullet points justifying an MSM.

Our Marine JAG has been going to Combat Stress after the mortar attack on his room. He is still shaken up. Specialist Campbell, whose bed the mortar literally landed on, is okay. I guess everyone handles stress differently. Our Marine JAG is worried about being off tomorrow. He asked me today, "What is a good officer?" and if I thought he was a good leader, etc. MSgt. Brown and I talked to him. He is very liberal in his views and not religious, which is unusual for a member of the military. I told him it is good that he vocalizes his disagreement on issues but "serving" your country or "serving" in the military means you submit to someone else's orders. I explained that it is okay to have new ideas or express ideas you think are better, but in the end, you still have to do as your superior officer directs you.

He and MSgt. Brown argued in the office yesterday over the Marine JAG wanting to assist a client who felt like her recruiter lied. MSgt. Brown told him it was outside the realm of legal assistance. The Marine JAG told MSgt. Brown, "You are always obstructing what I'm trying to do." MSgt. Brown asked if he could speak to him outside. I was on the computer and had to get off to see what was going on. I opened up the doors and called Lt. Larsen in to tell me what was going on. I went outside and talked to both MSgt. Brown and the Marine JAG. MSgt. Brown was right, and I explained to the Marine JAG why he couldn't advise the client on such a matter due to a conflict with command. He finally agreed and we pressed on.

I did learn more about the mortar that hit our living area. The insurgents fire from an area out beyond the overpass on the highway. That way, the overpass obstructs the towers at Abu from seeing them and the insurgents can use the overpass to aim at Abu....pretty sneaky.

January 27, 2005. Thursday

Well, I saw Peter Jennings today in the dining facility. I took a couple of pictures. No time to get a picture with him.

Dr. Sam, our interpreter, just walked up to him and blocked him from entering the door and started engaging in conversation with him. [Peter Jennings died from lung cancer 6 months later. He wasn't diagnosed until 3 months after his visit. He was an anchor of *ABC World News Tonight* from 1983 until his death].

TENSIONS FLARE

I had about 100 files to read today. I had other projects to work on, too, so I told the guys there were files in my office for them to review and to go in and get them. I then told them again about 4:45 pm. Finally, I told them if they wanted to go "home" at 5:30 pm then all the files had to be finished. They just hemmed and hawed around until they finally realized that I wasn't kidding. They started getting ready to leave at 5:30 pm. I believe it was one of the paralegals who said something about leaving and MSgt. Brown said the Major said no one leaves until the files are finished. Then people came into my office and started reviewing files.

I went to the gym tonight to make up for missing yesterday.

Well, I was supposed to be off today, but I just slept until 8 am and got to the office about 8:30 am. Of course, once I'm in there, there is work to be done, cases to review, taskings from Camp Victory, etc., so I just stay and work. Now, the new process changes require us to serve written notices to the detainees that we are going to prosecute. The Magistrate Cell serves notice on the detainees stating they are going to the CRRB. Now, if I decide they should be prosecuted, then I have to go out to the camp and serve notices.

One of the interpreters, Ahmed, asked me to write a letter of recommendation/appreciation for him. I wrote it to "To Whom It May

Concern," per his request, and said what a great job he has done. I found out that Ahmed's name isn't really Ahmed and Dr. Sam's name isn't really Dr. Sam. They don't use their real names out of fear the Iraqis will learn who they are and threaten them or their families. There is a $100,000 bounty on the heads of interpreters. We get cases all the time about detainees killing interpreters. I'm told the interpreters make $100,000 for 6 months of work. Something else. The files we get from TF 626, the special ops folks, have an apprehension form signed by a person using the pseudonyms of Frank something and Shane O'Conner. We learned that they are the same person and it is a female. Interesting.

I worked my "traps" out heavy tonight at the gym and can already feel my neck getting sore. I'm still up to 145 lbs. I did want to gain 10 pounds when I only weighed 135 lbs. I just want it to be muscle, not fat.

January 28, 2005. Friday

Not much going on today. We had a base-wide force protection exercise today to see how we could respond to a VBIED blowing through the wall and mortars landing. It lasted for about five hours. I had a couple of cases the new boss wanted. Colonel Beck, who is replacing Colonel Phelps, was working on an issue in which the Deputy Prime Minister of Iraq was asking MG Brandenburg about. The cases involved these two guys who were caught in two cars with a couple of AK 47s. They were caught in an area near a patrol that was hit with small arms fire and an RPG. The cars couldn't be positively identified as firing at the patrol, so we couldn't prosecute the guys.

The law in Iraq allows each adult male to carry one AK 47, so that wasn't illegal. I had to draft a memo explaining the two cases and send it to Colonel Beck who gave it to MG Brandenburg. Colonel Beck said MG Brandenburg was impressed with the documents and how fast I got it to him. He was going to actually give it to the Deputy Prime Minister of Iraq. Wow!

The NIPR was down all day so no email to/from family and no internet. I had to coordinate a plan to get Technical Sergeant Thomas to BIAP so he could redeploy home.

Some of the guys have been dragging butt. I had to tell them twice before we left tonight that we needed to empty the trashcans. They just stood there. I had to tell them again in a more serious tone. It's a lot different running an office in a combat zone than it is back home. I currently have four attorneys and five paralegals at the Abu office, and if you count that I am responsible for the Magistrate Cell, then that is an additional two attorneys, one paralegal, one cop, and two translators. Sometimes, you have to be stern. Asking nicely or jokingly doesn't always convey the urgency or seriousness of completing the task. I have learned a lot about leadership since I've been here. I heard a quote today. It goes something like... "Amidst a joke lies the truth." So, someone may be kidding when they say something, but they are also serious.

Seven days before I leave Abu! I'm ready to turn over leadership. I try to encourage the guys to go out and get things done. Like Lt. Faulkner who is gung ho about force protection. But sometimes I think he takes it too far. I try not to say too much to him about it because I don't want to discourage him. Then, the Marine JAG, I try to keep pumping him up because he always thinks he is a bad officer and leader and is failing. It is a very diverse group of people. I have the Marine JAG who says he is an atheist and Lt. Larsen who is a Mormon and they like to discuss religion or the lack thereof. I can hear them discussing religion on the other side of my office door. I let them go until I hear the conversation go from calm and rational to emotional and angry. Thank goodness I have some good NCO leaders, such as MSgt. Brown, Technical Sergeant Thomas, and Staff Sergeant Bascombe. They are always trying to find things to do. They are a good example for Specialist Campbell who will be promoted to Staff Sergeant on Sunday.

ELECTION WITH A BANG

January 30, 2005. Sunday

Election Day in Iraq! I was woken up at 6:30 am to a gunfight between the tower and insurgents. I shouldn't be surprised because this is what we predicted. I got to the office at 7:40 am, and 15 minutes later, multiple explosions shook our building. It was so loud! Then, the sirens sounded, and we put on our body armor...gunfire was still going off. Only Specialist Campbell and I were in the office but we still manned our fighting positions. The other guys assigned to our office were stuck in the dining facility. After about 30 minutes, the command center announced the warning that several unexploded ordinances (called UXOs) were still lying around inside the perimeter. A 60mm mortar landed about 50 feet from our office. It peppered the port-a-potties and outside walls of our office with shrapnel. If that was the one that shook our building, then that was the 2nd loudest one I have heard since I've been here. I could only imagine what a 120mm would have sounded like. I feel sorry for whoever was in that port-a-potty.

MSgt. Brown and I got back to the living area at 6:30 pm. We were just taking off our body armor when an explosion went off and shook our rooms! I put my vest back on... actually I still had it on one arm. Then the radio came on and said that the explosion was outside our perimeter to the SW about one–two clicks which is about half a mile to one mile away. It's amazing how loud and strong the combustion is, even when they hit outside the base.

I realized this was my last weekend in Abu. I will start packing on Thursday and leave on Friday for Camp Victory. The laundry I turned in on the 28th (Friday) is usually back within three days, but they have stopped all civilian travel because of an increase in attacks during the Iraqi election. My laundry is still sitting in the back of a truck at Abu. I guess I will be lucky to get it back before I leave since there are like 300–400 bags of laundry ready to go out. I won't be able to turn in anymore laundry like I wanted to do tomorrow because of the restriction on travel. The laundry can't leave Abu to get cleaned. I will just have to wear extra cologne.

February 1, 2005. Thursday

A few more gunfights and mortars in the distance today. No sirens. I washed some clothes today in one of the old funny-looking washing machines outside our living area. I'm still a couple of underwear short unless my laundry comes back tomorrow or Thursday. I have wet clothes hanging everywhere. About the election on Sunday, it was where Iraqis selected a 275-person congress. About 8 million Iraqis voted, which is 70% of the eligible population. That's impressive.

Last night, four detainees were killed at Bucca. They rioted after a military policeman allegedly tore a page in a Quran. They shot all their non-lethal rounds at the detainees. Only four detainees were killed. We had to get one of the detainee's files and summarize it for MG Brandenburg because that detainee was killed. Today, the new Staff Judge Advocate, Colonel Beck, asked who in our office had top-secret clearances. We are catching a lot of intermediate al-Zarqawi associates, so we are going to imbed a JAG with TF 626, special ops team, to mirror up the intel with evidence for the prosecution and threaten the associates with trial by the Iraqis if they don't cooperate with catching al-Zarqawi. Lt. Wall, the Navy JAG in my office, is the only one with top-secret clearance, but he has a Red Cross emergency request to return home because his mother-in-law, who lives with him, needs surgery. It probably won't get approved because they need him on that mission with TF 626. If he goes home on an emergency, they will tack on the time he is gone to the U.S. to the end of his tour. I also had to pick who should be the officer in charge when I leave and who to send to Camp Victory to present the cases to the CRRB. Our Marine JAG is the logical choice to go to Camp Victory because Lt. Larsen will be here only 45 more days and Lt. Faulkner can be OIC at Abu when I leave. But the Marine JAG doesn't adapt well to change and will probably freak when he has to travel in the red zone three times a week for the CRRB. He will also have to learn to be more succinct when he briefs the cases to the board, based on the length of his prosecution memos. That will leave two JAGs at Abu when I leave. Also, Lt. Larson knows computer stuff which will be needed to access the database for files when MSgt. Brown leaves Abu on the 7th of Feb. Of course, the Marine JAG has a female doctor he has hooked up with while at Abu. So, it was a tough call. It's funny how a mortar goes off in the green zone three miles away from the embassy and it gets all this news attention because that is where all the media is staying. No one sees or hears about Abu getting all these attacks all the time. Oh well. MG Brandenburg extended all the Air Force security team at the embassy for another tour because their replacements aren't here. I don't think I will get extended because Lt. Wall or Faulkner can fill in my job and we are closing our office.

PART III

HEADING HOME

COMING HOME

February 7, 2005. Monday

Well, I got to Camp Victory Thursday, February 4th, instead of Friday, February 5th as planned. Camp Victory called my office at Abu about 8:30 pm Wednesday, February 3rd, and said to bring some files that MG Brandenburg wanted. They said for me to come in to stay, too. I packed really quickly and left the next morning on Thursday, February 4th with all my stuff and the files they requested. The convoy had a five-ton truck with a body of a dead Iraqi in the back. Anyway, on Friday, February 5th, I ran around Camp Victory for five hours going to different offices to out process. One of the stops included a meeting/briefing with a physician and chaplain to make sure I was physically and mentally ready to return home. After all that running around getting papers signed at different offices, no one even asked for my paperwork before leaving BIAP.

I got up at 6 am Sunday, February 6th, and was picked up at 7 am by someone from the Camp Victory legal office. I ate breakfast and talked to Colonel Phelps. He was still in Iraq to have an overlap with his replacement, Colonel Beck. Colonel Phelps told me again how he put me in for a Bronze Star, but MG Brandenburg would probably not approve high awards to Air Force members because we are only deployed four months. The Bronze Star is given for either heroic achievement, heroic service, meritorious achievement, or meritorious service in a combat zone. Colonel Phelps thought I deserved one for meritorious service in a combat zone because I led a successful mission under almost daily attacks from the enemy. I was very honored to be nominated for a Bronze Star because, of 90+ medals, the Bronze Star is the 10th highest. The major whose slot I filled was deployed only three months and I was told he only received an achievement medal. My letter of evaluation hadn't been completed by Colonel Phelps and the award hadn't been approved by MG Brandenburg before leaving. They are supposed to be mailed to me.

Anyway, one of the guys from the Camp Victory legal office drove Staff Sergeant Shively, my paralegal from back home, and me to BIAP about 8 am. We tried to get on any earlier flights that had room instead of waiting until Monday for the flight for which we had reservations. Luckily, we were able to get an earlier flight. We were also lucky enough to find some seats in front of the TV on the plane. Transportation leaving Iraq was very different than arriving. I guess a lot had changed in the last four months.

While waiting for the plane to leave, we decided to go to Subway, which was operating out of a camper trailer. We waited an hour in line to get food from Subway for lunch and again for supper. It was kind of weird eating Subway sandwiches and hearing mortars exploding nearby. Mixing the comfort of home with the combat zone is really confusing to your mind.

Finally, at 7 pm, they announced for people who wanted to go to Ali Al Salem Air Base to come to the front of the tent. We were able to get on the flight out of Baghdad about 10:45 pm.

HITCHHIKING ACROSS KUWAIT

We landed at Ali Al Salem Air Base in Kuwait City, Kuwait at 12:15 am. The air base airport was only 25 miles from the border of Iraq. So far, it's been an 18-hour day. Upon landing, we unloaded our duffel bags and walked to a tent to inquire how to get to the Hilton Hotel in Kuwait City where we had reservations. We were told that we had to "make our way" to a bus stop and catch a bus at 2 am to get to Camp Doha, which is on the peninsula of Kuwait, near Kuwait City. It is about 45 miles away. Boy, this feels like hitchhiking.

At 2 am, we caught a bus that dropped us off on the side of the road at 3 am. It was dark, cold, and only a bus bench in the middle of nowhere. We were told to wait for a bus that should come by and pick us up at 6 am to take us to the Kuwait City Airport. Here I am in a strange foreign land, not understanding exactly where because it's been dark since I have landed. No one is around because it is in the middle of the night. I wasn't even sure I was on a military base. I still hadn't fully adjusted from being out of the danger zone of Abu, so it was a little unnerving.

Less than four hours ago, we were in Iraq where people were trying to kill us. Now, I am supposed to relax and sit on a bench at a bus stop like I am back in Oklahoma? It was so cold that I got out my sleeping bag, put it on a bus stop bench, and crawled inside to stay warm. Staff

Sergeant Shively put on his Gore-Tex jacket and decided to walk around to stay warm. Finally, the bus came by at 5 am and we got on it and waited. There were only three of us on the bus. At 6 am, the bus headed to the Kuwait City Airport, which is 20 miles away. On the way, we made a couple of stops and picked up more civilians.

We dropped one civilian off at the main terminal of the Kuwait International Airport, but Staff Sergeant Shively and I refused to get off there because we were in our uniforms and had our weapons. We hadn't been briefed on the rules or threat level. The airport is a regular civilian airport and we didn't believe the locals would take too kindly to U.S. soldiers walking in there wearing uniforms and carrying weapons. We could see several Kuwaiti military or civilian police inside the terminal. Perhaps I was being a little paranoid, but it was too soon for me to feel safe in my current environment. We told the bus driver we were not getting off the bus. I started closing the curtains that were on the bus so no one could see military uniforms onboard. I had the bus driver pull around to the back of the airport where the U.S. military planes were parked. It felt safer to be in an area with military assets.

Staff Sergeant Shively and I hurriedly exited the bus and ran inside a nearby office we believed supported the military planes. Inside, we saw an office where American contractors were working. We asked to use their bathroom to change out of our uniforms and into civilian clothes. We only had one or two changes of civilian clothes we had brought with us for this type of incident. Of course, they had been stored in my bags for the last four months. We explained to the guys that we needed to get to the Hilton Hotel in Kuwait City. One of the civilian contractors was nice enough to drive us around to the main entrance of the airport where the bus driver had originally tried to drop us off. This time we would be wearing civilian clothes and our weapons would be tucked into bags. The contractor used his cell phone to call the Kuwait City Hilton and asked them to send a car to pick us up. He stayed with us for the few minutes it took the hotel shuttle to arrive. A suburban showed up and drove us to the hotel where we arrived at about 8:30 am.

TO THE HILTON HOTEL, PLEASE

It was stressful riding across Kuwait City to the hotel in a car driven by two locals that I didn't know while trying to keep an eye on the suburban with all our luggage. I still don't want to get kidnapped or shot. Your mind tells you that you are still in danger, locals are threats, and you should prepare to fight. But your eyes see civilian buildings and cars. Things are pretty and colorful. It is really an adjustment.

At the entrance to the Hilton property, Kuwaiti soldiers searched under the cars for bombs and under the hood, too. Kuwait is flat and nothing to see just like Iraq. However, Kuwait does have lots of green grass, unlike Iraq where no grass seemed to exist.

The U.S. government had put us up in a villa at the hotel. It had two bathrooms, a living room area, couches, four separate bedrooms, washer and dryer, a kitchen, and a patio that led to a beach on the Persian Gulf. It was really awesome. Palm trees and all. The hotel gave us meal cards so we could eat for free. It was a buffet. We had salmon, shark, lamb, smoked trout, and outrageous amounts of other food and dessert. It was really fancy with syrup design garnish on the plates. Sergeant Shively and I decided to treat ourselves to the spa. We each got a one-hour massage. Then used the indoor pool, sauna, steam room, and Jacuzzi. It was 22 Kuwait dinars. The exchange rate is one dinar for about $3 U.S. It's a five-star hotel and very expensive. The prices in the shops are outrageous. We just realized it was 7:15 pm and we have been up for 37 hours without going to bed. Holy crap! Just a couple of cat naps here and there on the bus.

Walking around the hotel property was a little unnerving. I can actually walk outside without my body armor and helmet and weapons for the first time in four months! I put my pocket knife in my back pocket because I still didn't trust anyone and felt vulnerable without my rifle in my hand, my pistol on my hip, and body armor. All these men walking around in man-dresses. I still don't know who to trust. At least I haven't heard any mortars here.

The only civilian clothes I had was a short-sleeved shirt, which was too cold for the Persian Gulf in February. I didn't want to go too far, but I did want to see the area around the hotel. I walked down the beach of the Persian Gulf until I saw a convenience store up towards the highway. They sold shirts, so I bought a long-sleeved shirt with words I don't understand. I was also able to collect seashells from the beach and take some home. I guess you could say I was still collecting souvenirs.

Tomorrow, the last shuttle to the airport is 10 pm but our plane doesn't leave until 4 am. It will be another long night. We share our villa with an English guy who is going to Kirkuk, Afghanistan, and a civilian from Maumelle, AR on his way back to Baghdad. Well, I'm kind of tired and need to wind down before I go crazy.

THE LONG FLIGHT HOME

February 10, 2005. Thursday

 I don't really know the date. It's been a long day. I woke up at 10:30 am in Kuwait on Tuesday, then the shuttle came at 10 pm to take us to the airport. The plane didn't leave until 5 am. We took a five-hour flight to Aviano Air Base, Italy, on a commercial aircraft that was contracted out to the government. We were able to get off the plane for a couple of hours. We had to stay inside the airport terminal on base, but we could see the white-capped mountains from inside the airport. We loaded back up and flew one hour to Frankfurt, Germany, where we stayed about one hour in the terminal. I had already bought my souvenir refrigerator magnet four months earlier at this same airport, while on my way to Iraq, so I didn't need to purchase anything while there. We eventually got to reboard the plane and flew to Baltimore, MD.

 It was a nine and half hour flight from Germany to Baltimore. We landed about 2 am Iraqi time. It took two and a half hours to get our baggage from the airplane because the baggage people only brought a handful of bags at a time and only had two conveyor belts plus a ramp. Because we returned to America with about 250 people on the plane and the slow baggage handlers, most of us missed our connecting flights. We missed ours. Another day without seeing my family. I was so close to seeing my wife and kids tonight. It is a disappointment, but that is why you have to control your emotions and not get your hopes up.

The American Airlines counter closed at 7 pm and was just closing as we arrived. Luckily, they gave us a hotel voucher and a free meal ticket. The next flight out is tomorrow at 6:24 am to Dallas but the ticket counter opens at 4 am. We plan to leave the hotel at about 3:30 am... five and a half hours from now. I have been up for about 45 hours with only cat naps. I guess adrenaline keeps you going and won't let you sleep too long because in the back of your mind you don't feel safe. It is now 7 am Thursday Iraqi time and I've been up since 10:30 am Tuesday. Things feel weird. Everything is shaky. It could be the lack of sleep, or 15 hours on an airplane, or a mixture of both. I'm tired but had a nice steak as my free meal, courtesy of American Airlines. I just took a shower and found "somewhat" clean civilian clothes to wear tomorrow. Now, I'm going to try to go to sleep but not sure I can.

CONCLUSION

That was my last note in the journal. We did catch the plane from Baltimore to Dallas and Dallas to Oklahoma City, then a bus to Altus, OK, where our families met us. It was such a great feeling to be home and hugging my wife and children. It is hard to relax even though you know you are home where it is safe. It is an adjustment from being on guard/alert constantly to just being carefree. I did receive my award in the mail shortly after arriving home. It was a Bronze Star awarded for meritorious service under constant danger. My parents and my sisters came and visited me on the weekend I came home. It was a great visit and a relief knowing they didn't have to worry about me anymore.

Unfortunately, my dad passed away unexpectedly two weeks after my return. I try not to think about missing the last Christmas that my entire family would celebrate together, but I was able to talk to them on the phone while they were celebrating Christmas at my sister's house. I guess when you miss both of your kids' and wife's birthdays and your sister and dad's birthday, and the last Christmas with your dad, you sit back and realize you have really lived the Air Force motto…service before self. When most people think of military attorneys and war, they probably don't think about us being in harm's way. Hopefully, this book will provide a new perspective of JAGs in war.

PROLOGUE

AFGHANISTAN

Five years later, I was told my number was up for a second time. I was worried my luck couldn't hold up a second time. In fact, I was darn right confident I wouldn't make it back.

Since my deployment to Iraq, my professional life had soared, but my personal life had taken a drastic turn. On the professional side, I had been awarded the Bronze Star for my time in Iraq and I was working at my dream job. I was a medical law/medical malpractice defense attorney for the Air Force in Washington D.C. There were only eight of us. We were also responsible for advising 15 regional attorneys around the world on medical law and conducting physician adverse privileging hearings around the country.

In my personal life, I had suffered through a divorce in which my children were to be 2,000 miles away from each other and a parent. My daughter was living with her mother and I spent four years as a single dad to my eight-year-old son. But things were looking up. I remarried in January 2010 and was living in Northern Virginia. My daughter had started college in Oklahoma, and I sat in my ideal job in Washington, D.C.

HERE WE GO AGAIN

It was the spring of 2010 when I received the news. I had to deploy to Afghanistan for a six-month tour. On top of that, I was going to leave in December 2010 and miss the first Christmas with my new family. If I thought my son would have a tough time adjusting to a stepmother and two stepsiblings under the age of seven, he would now have to adjust and survive for six months without me helping him. His nearest relative was still about 1,500 miles away. He would turn 13 years old by the time I left, so I gave him the option to go live with his mom while I was gone for six months or to stay with his new stepmom and be with his friends. He took some time to decide because he wanted to be around family in the event something happened to me; however, it was also important that he continue his life with his friends as normal. That is what he did.

When I received the notice, I was hoping I was going to Kabul and not one of the smaller outposts around the country. I felt Kabul would be the most interesting, and the only town in the country that I could actually pronounce.

SORRY, WRONG COUNTRY

From the beginning, my trip over to Kabul was screwed up. The written directions we received are that when deploying to Kabul you must travel through Kuwait City, and if you are deploying to Iraq, then you go through the country of Qatar. When I was out processing for my deployment, I informed the military travel office of this directive. However, they insisted that my orders directed me to travel through Qatar. Being a good soldier/airman, I saluted smartly and carried on.

When I arrived in Qatar, it looked the same as it did seven years earlier. There was the pavilion where people sat outside and talked. I wasn't interested in a beer card this time. I was only interested in getting to my final destination. As I looked for someone who could tell me what day the flight to Kabul departed, they directed me to the base airport. I showed the people at the airport counter my military orders and they gave me a time and date to have my bags ready to go. I was only there for a day or so. I arrived at the airport and reported in to wait for my flight. I still didn't feel comfortable because I was in the wrong country and I felt that I may not actually get to the correct destination. I asked the front desk at the airport what time "my flight to Kabul" would land. They looked at my paperwork and told me that I was booked on the flight to Iraq! I kept telling them my orders said Kabul, which is in Afghanistan. They were baffled. I was baffled because after all, the military has been booking these trips for over 10 years. They should have the process worked out. Apparently, not.

It took the folks in charge several minutes to figure out what had happened and how I ended up in Qatar instead of Kuwait. Finally, they cracked the code. A deployment order number is assigned to each person. It tells everyone where you are going and when, etc. The deployment number I had been assigned had been reissued too soon. When my deployment number was entered into the system, it thought I was the previous person who had the number, and apparently, that person was sent to Iraq. There I am, in the wrong country, and only minutes away from ending up in the wrong combat zone!

Luckily, before I got on the plane, the issue was corrected, and I was able to board the plane to Kabul.

JUST CATCH A RIDE, THEY SAID

Upon landing at Kabul airport, I walked into the small building to await my bags. After locating my three large green bags with my clothes and equipment, I looked for the phone number of the military base where I was to be assigned. The base was called Camp Eggers, which I later learned was known as Camp Cupcake. The story I heard was it was given the name because of the many generals and senior officers that live there, which comes with nicer everything. I located the phone number of the office and called. The person who answered told me that I would have to "catch a ride" from the airport to Camp Eggers the best I could. Let me remind you, this isn't a small airport in some safe city. And, "catch a ride" only makes sense if you are in a town where you know people or in a time in which Lyft had been created, or, oh yeah, it is not a combat zone. How am I to catch a ride with three large bags, a rifle, a pistol, and a large rifle case, oh, and of course my body armor? I'm not going to be an easy passenger. That was the other issue. If I ever found someone going to my camp, they needed to have room for all my stuff. When deploying by yourself, you don't usually have the support you need.

I grabbed all my stuff and pulled it outside the front doors of the airport. I literally mean pulled. Dragged would be more accurate. They were heavy bags and not easy to pick up. It was December and it was cold. I had my large jacket to keep me warm. I sat outside on my bags and watched armored SUVs pull up and leave. Each time, I would ask the guys in the trucks where they were headed. Of course, no one is going where I needed to go. I started this "catch a ride" task at about 3 pm and I sat there until dark waiting. At last, about 6 pm, I found an SUV with armor on the sides and bulletproof glass that was only carrying three guys and they were heading to my camp. That means they had room for me and my stuff. I was grateful and hungry.

The truck traveled about five miles through the city of Kabul to get to my camp. We pull up, get through the main gate. Naturally, the truck I was in wasn't permitted inside the camp itself. It was dark, I was in a camp where I didn't know where anything was located. I guess I should explain what I mean by "camp." It was approximately 10 square blocks of a Kabul neighborhood that the U.S. built a fence around and called it a camp. I couldn't carry all my bags all around the neighborhood looking for the legal office. The guys who had given me a ride couldn't wait. They unloaded my bags and left. Luckily, there are no thieves among the military folks there. Theft is one of the worst offenses a military member can commit because if you can't trust a person with your property then how can you trust them with your life? I was able to grab my weapons and start walking with one of my bags to look for the legal office.

I walked several blocks, stopping and asking, stopping and asking. I finally arrived outside the legal office. Then, I walked back and made three trips bringing my bags up to the door. Worn out, tired, hungry, and a little worried about my safety was outweighed by the giddiness and relief of finally arriving. I walked in, met my boss, and was told I would be assigned to an office across the camp. WTF! Fine, but I would like to find a place to sleep and food to eat. I was directed to the building that was responsible for finding newcomer's places to stay until they could be assigned to a permanent location. I was given a bed in a room on a second floor that shared the space with no less than 10 other bunk beds. After dropping off my bags, still trusting that military folks would look after one another and not steal my stuff, I went to find food. I was able to find a dining hall where I could eat. It was free of course. No complaints. I was told to come back to the legal office the next day to get started.

The next day, I met other attorneys at the legal office. One was an Army Lt. Colonel who was heading back to the States for some R and R because he was deployed for a one-year term. He was assigned a room in a metal building that had its own bed and bathroom. It was about half the size of a college dorm room, but it was more comfortable than staying in an overcrowded room. He told me that I could stay in his room while he was back in the States for a couple of weeks. By the time he returned, I would have been assigned my permanent quarters. It felt good to catch a break.

The folks in the office across the camp where I was to be assigned came to the main legal office to meet me. They helped me carry my bags to my temporary living quarters. I met the rest of the folks assigned to my office. There was a Navy Commander JAG in charge and a Navy deputy. Can you believe the Navy deputy was one of the attorneys working in the Mag Cell when I was deployed to Abu Ghraib, Iraq? Then five Army, Navy, and Air Force attorneys, three paralegals, four Afghan civilian attorneys, and one Afghan translator. There I was informed that the mission was to help the attorneys for the Afghanistan police understand the new laws, some written by Italy, determine which laws should be changed, and establish a more efficient office. My specific role was to serve as the legal advisor/mentor to Mr. Roshangar, the Afghan legal advisor to the Afghanistan Minister of Interior. Wow! This will be exciting for a guy from Arkansas.

THAT'S NOT MY NAME

Mr. Roshangar didn't speak English. Therefore, I would speak to him through a translator. The other three guys with me would wait while I conducted business, the same as I do when they meet with their counterparts. About four months into my daily visits with Mr. Roshanger, the guys told me I had been mispronouncing his name. His name is pronounced "Russian-Gar" and the boy from Arkansas had been pronouncing it "Row-Shang-Her." I started thinking he doesn't speak English so he wouldn't know, right? But everyone recognizes their own name. Maybe that was the reason he always smiled.

Daily, four of us and a translator would load up in an armored Toyota Land Cruiser and drive across Kabul to two different locations. The main location was the Minister of Interior's compound, then there was a compound with a jail where we worked with an Afghan police legal advisor. My first trip out of the camp was very interesting. If I thought Iraq was a ghetto, well Afghanistan was the ghetto after it had been raided and bombed. The daily drive was through the traffic with locals driving and walking and just carrying on in the normal, everyday activities. It was a little unnerving being stuck in bumper-to-bumper traffic. We would never have allowed that to happen in Iraq, but this was a different type of war. This was an "I'm here to help" type of war; about winning the minds and hearts of the local people. Therefore, we followed the traffic laws. That didn't mean we weren't vigilant about our safety or that we didn't react when we were attacked with cinder blocks being thrown at the vehicles.

ANOTHER STINT IN PRISON

Not long after I arrived in Kabul, I was notified that I would spend 30 days in Bagram Air Base as a legal advisor to the detainee hearings. I will give you a little background so you can have a better understanding. The detention facility in Parwan is Afghanistan's main military prison. It houses foreign and local combatants/terrorists. It has been used longer and has handled more detainees than the U.S. Guantanamo Bay (GITMO) detention camp. In June 2011 it held over 1,700 prisoners. Without getting too technical, they were classified as unlawful enemy combatants and not POWs. The Enemy Combatant Review Board Tribunals were established to determine whether these unlawful enemy combatants pose a threat to coalition forces.

A hearing would consist of bringing the prisoner into the room where approximately five U.S. military officers sat as hearing officials. As the legal advisor to the Review Board Tribunal, my job was to ensure the procedures of the fair process were followed. There was a translator for the prisoner. The prisoner was allowed to bring in witnesses if they wanted to. It was more akin to the panel asking questions about the circumstances in which the detainee was captured to assess whether he was a security threat.

At the risk of making light of a prisoner's due process hearing, the detainees were often…comical.

In one hearing, the detainee asked to call his brother on the phone as a character witness. The brother asked the prisoner how he was? The prisoner said he was great. He has a nice bed, gets fed three times a day, and has time to exercise and pray. The prisoner's brother responded, "Just stay there, then. You have it better than me." The delay in the translation didn't take away from the humor. The detainee was not pleased with his witness.

DOING MY TIME

After 30 days, I returned to Kabul and continued mentoring/advising the Minister of Interior's legal advisor on various issues, such as hiring new attorneys, creating, and managing their personnel records, training, and winning the trust of the Minister of Interior. I attended meetings with Mr. Roshangar to observe him in action. He was a little shy or reserved, but, as time went on, he did a great job.

I didn't keep a journal during my time in Afghanistan, so I won't attempt to describe in detail the experiences as I remember them, such as the time I had to pull my handgun on an Afghan policeman who forced us to open our car door placing the lives of all in the vehicle in danger; or drive down crowded streets while locals threw rocks at the window of our vehicle; or practice unholstering my handgun from a seated position because there had been a few incidents of U.S. soldiers getting shot while inside offices mentoring the local leaders, like we were doing.

I made it home from Afghanistan safe and healthy. I picked back up where I left off in my personal and professional lives. Even today, when people ask me about my deployments, they often say, "You were not in a dangerous place because you are an attorney." I just smile and realize their view of military attorneys is marred by their perspective of the comforts enjoyed by civilian attorneys stateside. Military attorneys, chaplains, and physicians are in harm's way when they deploy. They may not be kicking down the doors or defending outposts like the brave soldiers do, but they perform their duties, whatever those may be. Everyone's experience is different and all sacrifice for the love of our country.

ABOUT THE AUTHOR

Hugh Spires, Jr. is a father, grandfather, attorney, and veteran. He served 28 years in the military—eight years in the infantry, and 20 years as an attorney in the Air Force. He retired from the Air Force in 2015 and practices in Dallas, Texas. He often has a funny story or a dad joke to tell and recently wrote a rhyming ABC book for his grandchildren, who may or may not be excited about it.

Made in United States
Orlando, FL
14 October 2023